SO YOU WANNA BE AN

ALL STAR

SO YOU WANNA BE AN ALL STAR

BECOME THE CLEAR PROMOTION CHOICE

JARED HAMILTON

JWH PRESS

JWH
PRESS

JWH Press Books may be purchased for educational, business or sales promotional use. Visit www.hamiltonexecutivecoaching.com

Production and creative provided by Epiphany Creative Services
Printed in the United States of America
Library of Congress Cataloging-in-Publication Data
Library of Congress Control Number: 9798993245980
FIRST EDITION
Jared Hamilton – 1st ed.
TITLE: So You Wanna Be an All-Star: Become the Clear Promotion Choice
p. cm.

ISBN: Hardcover: 979-8-9932459-0-4
ISBN: Paperback: 979-8-9932459-8-0
ISBN: eBook: 979-8-9932459-4-2

1. BUSINESS 2. Careers 3. Career Advancement & Professional Development

Distributed by JWH Press
26 10 9 8 7 6 5 4 3 2 1

This book is dedicated to my wife, Whitney, who unconditionally loved, prayed for, supported and encouraged me throughout all my "errors" on the way to the All-Star level.

I love doing life with you, babe.

CONTENTS

FOREWORD

Clint Pulver
President, Center for Employee Retention
Emmy Award-winning Speaker and Author

Every great career has a spark—one moment when someone realizes they're not just here to punch a clock. They're here to matter. It's the moment a professional decides they're ready to move from contributing to transforming, from doing their job to actually owning their impact.

After sitting across from thousands of employees in my undercover work, I can tell you this: the people who rise aren't always the loudest, the most polished, or the most technically gifted. They're the ones who pay attention to the small moments—the details, the initiative, the quiet trust-building most people overlook.

That's one of the reasons Jared Hamilton stood out to me when we first met. He attended one of my keynote speeches, and after the presentation we shared one of those quick, meaningful small moments—the kind you don't plan, but you walk away remembering. A week later, we jumped on the phone and had a genuine conversation sharing our journeys and our purpose. And somewhere in the mix, thanks to a mutual appreciation for ridiculous socks, he sent me a pair of Texas-branded crazy socks that still make me smile.

That's Jared. That's who he is. Someone who shows up in the small moments—and helps others learn how to do the same.

This book is packed with those moments.

Throughout these pages, Jared breaks down the small shifts that separate a "pretty good employee" from the kind of professional teams fight to keep. The small behaviors. The small decisions. The small conversations that—over time—make you someone others rely on, trust, and remember.

If you're an employee reading this, you're going to see yourself in these pages. You're going to see where you've been playing small, where you've been waiting for permission, and where you've been underestimating the influence you already have. You'll learn how to create the kinds of moments leaders notice—moments that accelerate your career long before you ever receive a title.

And if you are a leader?

You'll feel this too. Because Jared lays out what your people need—the clarity, the mentorship, the human connection—that keeps them engaged and helps them thrive. You'll see the role you play in shaping these moments and why they matter.

In the end, this book is an invitation to elevate your presence—whether you're on the rise or already guiding a team. To commit to the small things that build trust and culture. To take ownership of the only thing that truly separates the good from the unforgettable: the way you show up every single day.

Lean in. Pay attention to the moments. They're your pathway to becoming an All-Star.

INTRODUCTION YOU SHOULDN'T SKIP

The Key to Reading This Book

"Jared, you always have a better way of doing things, don't you?" my college baseball coach, Hadley Hicks, raged at me across the field, because I was loudly suggesting a different way of doing a drill. And I was a freshman. To this day, my former teammates will chastise me for this habit of mine to call out things I think I can make better.

Now, thirty years later, I can't seem to shake that habit, as in this book, I will be using what I believe to be a better way to communicate and what it takes for professionals in the workplace to perform at an elite level in a company and be the clear promotion choice in their organization. Or what I like to refer to as an All-Star. Having been in the corporate environment, and specifically human resources and people development work, for over a dozen years now, I'm not a fan of the way many people communicate what great performance is and the expectations of excellence in our companies. I feel compelled to share with you what I know it will take to skyrocket in your organization in a way that is *better* than anything you have received so far, with all due respect to Coach Hicks.

Some of the anecdotes and experiences I offer are based in business settings, but the concepts can be applied to most companies, firms, organizations, or institutions. I've worked closely with executives in various sizes of corporations, churches, academic institutions, among others. These skills transcend all kinds of workplaces. If you are in doubt about the value of any of them in your workplace, ask your senior leadership.

The term "Meets Expectations" is often used for "At Level" or "Satisfactory" in many corporate performance reviews or appraisals to describe how the professional performed in the most recent business cycle or quarter. This is typically done once or twice a year, some companies more often. When I was first exposed to the "Meets Expectations" score upon my entry into corporate America, I was reminded that in elementary school, when they scored behavior for the period, we either got an S (Satisfactory) or a U (Unsatisfactory). I got all S's during my elementary career! Somewhere along the way, performance appraisal "inflation" occurred. "Satisfactory" apparently didn't reward excellent behavior, so E's were introduced. This has apparently spilled over into the work environment with the desire to receive evaluation scores such as "Exceeds Expectations."

When being evaluated, so many professionals are offended if they get the equivalent of an S or a "Meets Expectations" because they want something more. Some blame this evolution on generational changes and participation ribbons. But let's be honest—has anyone ever used the phrase "Meets Expectations" outside the four walls of companies? When a favorite athlete makes an amazing play at the end of the game, do you ever hear someone say, "He is an 'Exceeds Expectations' player"? When you hear a musician playing live, do you ever comment and say, "That was decent. They are a 'Meets Expectations' performer"? Those words and phrases aren't used by anyone outside corporate walls. They are corporate jargon, and it's time to use real words to describe the performance levels of professionals. Much like celebrities or athletes, everyone knows what a professional is and what an All-Star is. And that's what I desire for you to discover about yourself when reading this. No more jargon.

When I participated in any activity growing up, I didn't need a coach to tell me "how" I was performing. Coaches were there to help me perform better. The measurements (statistics) communicated how I was doing. In baseball, for example, we had errors, strikes, outs, hits, and averages that communicated our level of performance. Comedians have audience laughter, or the lack thereof, to measure their success. Music artists have crowds that stay, follow, and ultimately buy. I believe professionals in the workplace can absolutely determine "how" they are doing if companies and their leaders resource them with the measurements. Then leaders can help them develop further instead of spending so much time trying to interpret and communicate the performance, hoping the employee agrees. I want this book to speed up this process.

I was blessed to accelerate rather quickly in corporate America after an unexpected exit from collegiate athletics. Unless you are legitimately retiring, the majority of exits from collegiate athletics are not 100 percent voluntary. Meaning you are usually not offered another contract or you are asked to resign. It's a softer way of getting fired, but it all feels the same, trust me. In 2011, I was asked to resign. Not because I lost games; in fact, I actually won a lot of games. I had resurrected my alma mater from a six-win season before I showed up to being a thirty-win-plus team. I was asked to leave because I didn't even meet the expected level of professionalism in some of the skills this book addresses—communication, relationships, and planning, to name a few—and I found myself having to rebound, up skill, and turn a corner.

Fortunately, I navigated the turn well, and now, fourteen years later I can attest to leveling up my skills that ultimately landed me in a C-level executive position. I have listened to many of my key executives describe the things they witnessed as I climbed up the organizational ladder and have additionally asked what they look for in professionals that makes them clear promotion choices. For the purposes of this book, I will call the employees who exhibit these high-level attributes the All-Stars. It's a much better label than "Exceeds Expectations."

Now, there are likely many niche professional skills needed to rise in the workforce, mostly technical in nature. These include accomplishing day-to-day tasks, software proficiencies, and meeting deadlines. But these are rarely the skills that make you an All-Star; they are the skills that keep you employed. The performance skills discussed in this book, if you adopt them, offer an incredible opportunity to fly high through an organization. This is likely a key reason some of you have received this book, through reference of one of your leaders. So take the hint. Hopefully, you will adopt the strategies, climb through your organization into leadership, then pass on this book to the next generation of potential All-Stars.

> DISCLAIMER: If you are unable to complete the technical day-to-day tasks of your job at a basic level, none of these concepts will ultimately help. You have to be able to do your current job tasks well if you want to have any chance of climbing the ladder. Whether it's finishing projects, meeting deadlines, creating pivot tables or sales pitch slide decks, etc., if you are not reliable with your day-to-day tasks, focus on those first. Finishing tasks is the foundational part of your job.

With my history in sports, namely baseball, I couldn't help but relate this topic of rising in business to the game I love by using the term *All-Star* to indicate someone who will fly up the company ranks among all the other professionals. Athletes who are paid for their skills are also called professionals, just like we are in the corporate world. And many sports professionals remain unknown because they aren't All-Stars. All-stars are statistically much better than their professional peers and receive a different level of attention and most of the time better remuneration. This can be analogous to any performance-based profession like singing or acting, and it works in the corporate world as well.

In each of the chapters to come, we will identify a specific skill and the following levels of performance in that particular skill.

> **All-star:** a level of employee who executes skills at a level that professionals either don't think or know about or want to achieve. All-stars are often trusted with critical, higher-level initiatives because of these skills.

Professional: the high level of performance at which a great majority of individuals in a company or organization perform. Professionals are paid for the skill they bring to the organization and the product they complete. They are reliable performers who consistently do what they are paid to do at a successful level. In many current corporate reviews, professionals' performance is described as "Meets Expectations" or "Average." And that is not an offensive label for performance; it is what professionals are paid for. And that is honorable, because "Below Average" would not be sustainable.

Developing: an early-in-career or entry-level employee or someone new to the industry or trade, learning mostly the technical components of their job, very likely making professional skill errors due to a lack of understanding of process, professionalism, or culture. Those who notice they don't meet even the professional level of performance for a particular skill discussed in this book are in the developing stage for that skill. Keep reading and growing. We won't necessarily talk about what skills developing people have or don't have, but if you are seeing you're not doing what even professionals do, this is where you are.

There are specific 'time-outs' during the chapters where we pause to give you moments of self-reflection to determine where you are already an All-Star or where you need to improve in a specific skill and some summative brief actions to get you ready to improve on them tomorrow. Look for the following:

Performance Point: Here are the measurements of performance. Throughout the book, these are questions for you to consider based on real experiences and scenarios I have gone through that offer point-in-time decisions we all have likely encountered or will encounter in our careers. I will stop whatever anecdote I am walking through and ask you a question to consider from a previous similar performance opportunity. Make sure you're honest with yourself during these types of self-evaluation exercises. And don't read ahead before truly answering these questions. You won't get the mileage from this book if you aren't real with yourself. If you have not experienced the situation the performance point references, then answer hypothetically but as honestly as you can to gauge your current tendencies. This is a moment where you will be able to define what level of performance (professional, All-Star, etc.) you have been performing at and identify how you can develop your skills.

Error Warning: Provided you desire to be an All-Star, the error warning will identify actions that fall short of being an All-Star. Error Warnings in this book normally follow Performance Point questions. All-stars very seldom make the errors identified in this book. Decisions characterized as "developing" will occasionally be highlighted, but it's assumed anything short of a professional approach is developing.

> DISCLAIMER: The errors mentioned in this book are not horrible or career ending; they're merely career limiting if regularly committed. All professionals, in sports or otherwise, make errors all the time, just fewer than others and often in tough circumstances. All-stars make far fewer of those errors. Most employees choose a professional path, and their performance points are done at a professional level, and organizations are very satisfied with the approach. Anyone can have a very good career with a professional approach, hence the term *professional*. Professionals are very good at what they do. If you take the professional approach consistently, you will remain a professional. You'll need to understand, however, that All-Stars fly up the organization. You can decide at any time to take your performance to an All-Star level.

Skill Self-Reflection: At the end of the chapter, there is a one-question survey for you to assess where you are in that particular All-Star skill.

The Closer – Bullpen Bullets: The "closer" of a baseball team is the pitcher who typically comes in (from the part of the field called the bullpen) at the end of a close game to finish the game. A friend and professional peer of mine suggested it would be helpful if there were short quick takeaways, or bullets, from the chapter. Sounds like the job of a closer. Appropriately, many corporate offices have open seating areas called "bullpens" where professionals and All-Stars work as well.

To exercise some personal accountability, at the end of the book, you can total your chapter scores in the final assessment to see where you are on your journey to achieving All-Star status! Sustaining professionalism or average performance is not what this book is designed to help you do.

So do you *really* want to be an All-Star? This book will help you find out by identifying key All-Star skills, determining the performance points you typically take, and helping you improve your mindset and decision-making ability in order to execute at an All-Star level.

If you want to work through this at an elevated level, gather a group of trusted peers to work through the skills and evaluations together to determine if they see you the same way you see yourself.

Regardless of how you begin and carry out this journey, an All-Star move is picking up this book and starting your journey of development. Make no mistake, this is a journey, and there is no point in which you feel finished—and that is the best part. The journey of improving and working on these skills will actually make you feel better about who you become more than whatever promotion you land. The promotion is just the icing on the cake. So I hope that through self-assessment and goal setting, you will decide what you need to develop and then begin to implement the All-Star skills covered in this book to vault you through your organization to the career you desire. I hope one day to hear about your journey to becoming an All-Star.

1

PRESENCE

At some point in a professional's career journey, they reach places where they get "on the radar." This means they did something that was *different* from their peer group—something advanced. Something more than what most professionals do. They made an All-Star move.

If a professional creates a pattern of this type of performance, that's when they're looked at for promotions and advancement—because their name keeps popping up for doing something more or different.

Professionals in an organization—those who consistently perform at a high level in their field—are great. They are necessary and valuable. They get the job done. Kim Scott, in *Radical Candor*, calls them Rock Stars.[1] And I've known some of the best professionals that I would have on my team any day. However, they also choose *not* to be All-Stars. They may be in a season of life where they don't want to focus on being an

[1] Kim Scott, *Radical Candor: Be a Kick-Ass Boss Without Losing Your Humanity* (New York: St. Martin's Press, 2017).

All-Star, or they may have different overall life or career goals. They also may not line up for the next promotion, if it's leadership related, because they understand that they have *chosen* to be a valued professional. In those cases, my hat is off to them.

One of the best professionals I worked with, Don, was what some companies call an "individual contributor." This gentleman was far more talented than I. And I was his *boss*! He never hesitated to tell me that he loved what he did for his eight hours of the day. He got out of leadership years before I worked with him, and he never wanted back in. (He had owned his own company.) He told me never to ask him about promotions or getting back into leadership. He was in the job he wanted to do as an individual contributor and desired no more.

I respected that so much. And even more, he never hesitated to give me advice when I asked for it. That, my friends, is a *professional*. Make no mistake, though—Don was not an All-Star. And companies are looking for someone to promote through the organization who have a presence and desire to go beyond their current role.

So before moving on with this read, you should decide if you want to be like Don and be the professional or if you want to make a run for it and be an All-Star. This entire book is dedicated to giving you tangible skills and a way to assess them so you can make a decision if you really *wanna be an All-Star*.

As a kid, I grew up fond of books that were called "Choose Your Own Adventure" novels. A simple but brilliant concept of presenting a story, then offering two different decisions when a fork in the road was encountered, which was usually every two pages. Based on your decision, the book would take you to a certain page and your story would be different than if you had made the other decision. I will offer something very similar where we'll break from the anecdote or story from my own experience to allow you to reflect on what you would normally do or have done in the past.

A quick note to the more skeptical reader: One of the greatest anonymous audience survey critiques I received after I presented at a conference was, "Engaging speaker, but I don't know that I believe all his stories." I love that! A criticism that I took as the greatest compliment I could ask for. Apparently, some of my life is a little hard to believe, and I am okay with that, because as I share these stories, I often think, *I can't believe that happened*. But I can assure you, I am not that creative to make these up. And the key characters appearing in these stories are in the acknowledgments and can attest to them (and have read them already).

Let me digress no longer, and let's get going. But be prepared—the first thing this takes is an All-Star presence in your company. One of my mentors would always say to those wanting to be promoted, "Be a leader in place first." Another mentor would say, "Bloom where you're planted." Yes, a little corporate jargony, but what they are talking about is having a distinguishable presence in your company regardless of your job title.

And this isn't about good attendance. This is about having a *presence*—unique from and more prominent than that of your professional peers.

Very early on, when transitioning from my collegiate athletic career to the energy industry, I made a decision—after listening to countless leaders tell employees to "ask questions" and be curious—to be curious in every meeting or room I was in. If there was something I didn't understand completely, I would ask to learn more about it. And yes, I was terrified that other people would think I was annoying or dumb—but we were all encouraged to ask questions.

In my first year, after I had made my "curious" presence relatively known, there was a virtual training being conducted by the executive of the learning department. She was hosting the session through Zoom, and all the field employees who held my same position were gathered together in a training facility—about twenty of us—watching and listening to the trainer. I was intently listening and making sure I gave room for others in my group to discuss and ask questions.

The executive, however, likely unable to see every individual clearly through her monitor back at headquarters, suddenly barked out, "Where's Hamilton at? I haven't heard him open his mouth yet. Is he in this training?"

Some people might have melted down at that moment. But I knew then that I was off to a good start—when my silent presence, even for just a few moments, was noticeable to an executive.

PERFORMANCE POINT

Are you an active participant, engaged and consistently curious or inquisitive in meetings, trainings, or other in-office gatherings?

ⓘ ERROR WARNING

Professionals often check the box at trainings and meetings. They'll answer questions directly asked of them. All-stars are typically in seats closer to the presenter, listening actively, and often asking questions to clarify points or spur thoughtful additional discussion.

Before I lose all of the more introverted crowd here, please bear in mind one of the most iconic leaders in America's history had dynamic presence but was introverted. In Doris Kearns Goodwin's book about Abraham Lincoln, she highlights how Lincoln's calm, reflective demeanor and emotional intelligence helped him manage strong personalities, despite being personally reserved.[2]

You can do this.

The Customer Meeting

I was a few months into my career change from collegiate athletics to the corporate world. The energy company I was now with invited all operations front-line supervisors to the annual customer meeting. This was even prior to being known as the "curious" one in meetings. When I found out this customer meeting was taking place at a high-end convention center and resort in Kansas City, Missouri—and the entire chief executive team would attend—I realized this was a major event, not a mere meeting.

[2] Doris Kearns Goodwin, *Team of Rivals: The Political Genius of Abraham Lincoln* (New York: Simon & Schuster, 2005).

PERFORMANCE POINT

Do you shudder at the thought of going to a work-related function outside working hours, or do you get excited when you're invited to companywide events?

ⓘ ERROR WARNING

If you are on the path to All-Star, you have to change your perspective if you have a disdain for functions outside the "nine to five," whether you are going to own your own business or climb up the ladder in the one you're in. I'm not endorsing eighty-hour workweeks (all the time). I have a beautiful wife of twenty-six years and four awesome kids. I serve at my church, coach youth baseball, speak at HR conferences, and write. My "work and life" are amazing. I also just choose not to be a homebody, binge-watch Netflix, and doomscroll on Instagram. You can too.

Now, if your personality is averse to traveling or big crowds, any small personal or family conflict will tempt you as an excuse to avoid this type of event. In full transparency, sometimes I would consider reasons not to go. That's human. No one, especially post-COVID, will think less of you for canceling for health reasons—I don't know if that will ever change.

I'm not saying to abandon your family or health in critical moments. However, be honest with yourself. If you wouldn't cancel your trip to the tropics, or skiing, or the hot date you've been hoping for, then you're not performing at an All-Star level of presence if you skip out on corporate events claiming the same reasons; you are a professional at best if your work doesn't get the same dedication.

Ironically, it's often the same people who often have something "come up" that doesn't allow them to attend events. Is that you? Trust me—people notice, and it's the people who make the decisions on promotions who notice.

This is a tough error to talk about, and for that reason, it is the longest error warning in this book. But at the risk of offending the

> reader, all this needed to be said. This is a career enhancement and advancement book—helping you identify opportunities and maximize performance decisions and execution to get you to an All-Star level of performance. There will be more hard decisions ahead, but few as important as the presence you want to have in your company. Now, let's get back to the customer meeting.

With company events like our annual customer meeting, I learned that the typical process involves the customer service team sending out a list of confirmed attendees, both company employees and customers. As I reviewed the list, I was clearly going to be outranked by everyone in the room. This was a meeting I needed to prepare for—but I really didn't know how.

Although I had been to a few large connecting events in my past career as a baseball coach and felt relatively comfortable around a crowd, but the stakes were higher here. I called a mentor who was much more versed in these types of energy industry get-togethers. He called them "boondoggles."

His advice was surprising, but memorable: "There will be a lot of high-end liquor there, so if you drink, make sure you keep a good drink-to-water ratio. One water for every two beers or one water for every mixed drink. This is important, because someone is going to be the company idiot on Monday—make sure it's not you. Other than that, be *present*, meet people, and be yourself."

PERFORMANCE POINT

Would you have heeded the advice—or enjoyed the free drinks a little too much?

ⓘ ERROR WARNING

Many professionals commonly make a colossal error here and consider this a party where they can enjoy life and party on. When a company is expecting you to attend and paying for your travel expenses, meals, and room bill, don't let the event distract you from the fact that you are *still working*, even at midnight.

If you are curious, there ended up being a company idiot and he doesn't make the professional level here.

This turned out to be valuable advice from my mentor, as I ended up anything but the company idiot. The polar opposite would occur.

During a cocktail reception event with the customers on the eve of the formal meeting, the CEO of our company briefly mentioned his appreciation for my attendance and my engagement with our customers as he passed by me. He mentioned, under his breath, how he needed to get others from the company engaging with our guests in a similar fashion. I watched him walk over to a table of newer leaders sitting together at a table and seemingly lecture them for doing everything they could to stick to their beer and each other instead of meeting new people. When he finished talking and pointing, they reluctantly started working the room.

I knew enough about networking to know I needed to have a presence by walking around and finding ways to break into conversations. Typically, I would find people I knew from my company and organically say hello to them while they stood amid a crowd—then they would introduce me to the customer they were talking to. Oftentimes, after they would introduce me and I was comfortably conversing with the customer, that coworker would "leave us to it" and move to other customers. I learned years later there is a networking term for this called "bumping a conversation," very common for those in sales and other professional services during happy hours and networking events. As I worked the room later into the evening and "bumped" into various conversations, I was proud I was still putting coherent sentences together, having kept the H_2O flowing. There were plenty of others who I could tell did not heed a similar water ratio practice.

PERFORMANCE POINT

Do you stay in packs of only known people at work events, or do you like to venture out of your normal circles and build connections?

ⓘ ERROR WARNING

It's easy to get locked in with a familiar colleague talking about business when you're at events like this. But this is a professional move, not an All-Star move. At least professionals do not stand alone in the corner or figure out a way to leave early; those are amateur, or developing, moves.

The only way to grow your All-Star skills and get better at working a room is to *work rooms*. Save the conversations with your colleagues when you get back to the office in the morning. It's likely the colleague wanting to keep talking to you is doing so because they're a professional not wanting to be an All-Star or work the room either.

Much later in the evening of the reception, I found myself with a group of six customers from different companies; we had been talking sports, family, travel—the usual go-tos. There was some talk of the pipeline and the business of energy in general, but nothing earth-shattering. The serious stuff would be covered in the morning at a general session in the conference center.

With very little time left in the customer "happy hour" (it was almost nine p.m.), half of the room cleared out, and the bartenders began to put the liquor away. One of our customers, Patrick, asked the group, "Want to take this meeting over to the BBQ restaurant across the street?" The group nodded in agreement while Patrick looked my direction.

"You coming with us, Jared?" Patrick asked.

I started calculating the seven-thirty a.m. start we had the next morning and the odds I wouldn't be back in my room until extremely late. *I'm going to be exhausted. Plus, I'm not a big player here. I'm just an operations supervisor—not a business development or customer service executive. It's no harm done to call it a night. On the other hand, I'm pretty sure these are rather valuable customers to our company who just invited me out.*

PERFORMANCE POINT

Would you have opted for a good night's sleep or headed for some BBQ?

ⓘ ERROR WARNING

Passing up opportunities to display your presence, even for very understandable reasons, is extremely common as a professional. And choosing a good night's sleep here is not a wrong move, but All-Star moves are not the comfortable ones. Your opportunities will be vastly reduced if you don't take advantage of moments like this to build relationships, even moments that may cost you a few hours of sleep.

I confidently said to Patrick, "Of course, I'd love to." The networking opportunity was my main driver in making the decision—but we were also heading to one of the top BBQ places (and most expensive) in one of the best cities for BBQ in the world. I would be lying if that didn't help me feel better about my decision.

Sleep would have to wait. As we walked to the high-end BBQ restaurant, I quickly reviewed what my role would be here. *I have their business cards, they have mine, I'll make sure to continue to open up and build relationships—what am I missing?*

The BBQ bill. Remember, this is one of the most expensive places in Kansas City.

Wouldn't the company want me to pick this up? Being about six months into my job with the company, this was not my call to make, because this was easily going to be close to a $1,000 dinner. I knew we weren't going to McDonald's—and I was considering feeding a small army. I texted one of our customer service executives, quickly, hoping he would check his phone. I knew he was still closing out the party, working the room, when we left.

When I texted him that I was out to eat with a group of customers and wondered if I should pick up the bill, he texted back, "Who's with you?"

I texted back company names—not people names. I knew they were some of our biggest customers.

He quickly texted back, "YES!" And yes, it was in all caps and with an exclamation point.

During the dinner, I learned much more about Rob, Patrick, and "the Pams," as I sat closest to these individuals. The two women in the party who were both named Pam actually shared the same last name too—no relation, but it was fun to learn and, better yet, very easy to remember.

I learned about all my new connections' families, their interests, and what they each did during their workday. And with so much knowledge at the table, I asked as many questions as I could about natural gas trading, strategy, and how what I did from day to day was valuable to what they did.

PERFORMANCE POINT

In these situations, would you be asking questions, answering questions, or telling personal stories during the dinner?

ⓘ ERROR WARNING

Professionals will tend to talk about themselves a lot in these types of group environments, or, if more introverted, disappear into the wall, allowing the crowd to drive the conversation and not being "memorable," not having *presence*. All-stars are engaged, genuinely curious, and willing to ask open-ended questions.

From a technical perspective, this was an accelerated course on natural gas reliability and different types of natural gas contracts. From a relational perspective, I was building a list of connections I could easily pick up and call or shoot an email to when I had a question about the various aspects of the business.

Two hours later, I signed for the biggest dinner bill I'd ever signed for in my life. About six hours after that, my alarm went off to get ready for the morning meeting. It was a struggle—but I had enough coffee to survive the day.

By the end of the meetings that weekend, though, I had started friendships that would prove to be meaningful in the future. They will be a key piece of the experience I describe in chapter 9, "Planning."

For the Introverts

For those more introverted in nature, you may look at networking events—or just having a presence in general—as more difficult. However, there is still great opportunity where introverted personalities can excel. Matthew Pollard wrote a fantastic book called *The Introvert's Edge to Networking* that strategizes how to approach these types of meetings in ways that capitalize on an introvert's strengths.[3]

In short, approaching this event as a work product—and planning ahead by having your go-to stories and questions for others ready—helps establish and build your presence. I highly recommend reading this book if building connections and networking with others are not skills you have mastered. Lastly, many introverts I know are incredible listeners; much better than I am. This is a great advantage in the networking game.

Final Word on Presence

As I mentioned before, I was anything but the company idiot on Monday after the annual customer meeting. I was the rookie operations supervisor who somehow broke into a group of major customers during a company event, then got invited and subsequently scooped up a four-figure dinner tab and seven friends in the industry. As you can imagine, this was noticed at the highest levels of the company.

This helped my career stock—and some professionals would say I "caught lightning in a bottle." But review all the performance points

[3] Matthew Pollard, *The Introvert's Edge to Networking: Work the Room. Leverage Social Media. Develop Powerful Connections* (Hoboken, NJ: Wiley, 2020).

and error warnings along the way. If your work habits are similar, you'll find yourself *present* in a lot of storms with a lot of lightning and a lot of bottles. Keep catching! Furthermore, don't stop catching. One big win or bolt of lightning doesn't make a career or an All-Star.

This is not just about customer meetings or networking events. This is also the type of presence you should have in the office. One employee we have in our firm is typically one of the last to leave optional after-hours events because they are often seen helping out with cleanup and visiting with the last of us still hanging around, never looking like they are in a hurry to get out of there. This person happens to be an identified All-Star in our company with very high potential. But it goes far beyond taking out the trash a couple times. It's a consistent presence at corporate or office-related events or trips, professional trade conferences or symposiums. Presence can sometimes be felt because you are often nearby in the office at the most impactful moments and times, or even on an occasional Friday when most people are working from home (we'll talk about this more in chapter 10 – Friday Focus)—because you realize the potential value of being present.

Professionals often focus on when they can appropriately stop or leave. And please hear me, this is not a bad thing. It's just not an All-Star move. All-stars focus on when and where else they can be impactful and add value. Open your mind to all the places you can be present for your organization, and take advantage of them. Plenty of your professional peers will not.

Presence is likely the single most important skill you need in order to become an All-Star in your career, your life, and your community. You *have* some sort of presence. You have to assess what it is and what you want it to do for you.

Professionals typically have respectable presence—always on time, respectful, and knowledgeable. All-star presence is different. It requires belief, intentionality, planning, flexibility, and courage.

Many of the skills that follow in this book assume you are committed to being *present* as an All-Star.

All-stars believe they can create opportunity with their presence, so they seek those moments. Are you doing this?

Even at the risk of losing a reader, let me say this: If you aren't willing to assess and improve your presence where needed, the rest of this book will be largely ineffective, and you should invest your time elsewhere. That's the coach in me being honest with you.

Before making that decision, though, I'd challenge you to ask a successful executive, someone you trust, to read this chapter and answer the following questions: 1) Will "presence" as described in this chapter put you on an All-Star path? and 2) What is your current presence level—All-Star, professional, or lower than that? If you don't know a successful executive you can ask, then you have your answer to number 2 already and now know what you have to do.

Make a goal to improve your presence. Keep reading the chapters that follow—and let's get there.

Presence Self-Reflection

This self-evaluation is for *you*. If you want to share with a trusted peer or leader to build accountability toward your newly acquired skills, that is a bonus. At the very least, if you are choosing to make a run at being an All-Star, personal accountability can start here. Decide which number below applies most to you at this point and circle the number.

1. I've never recognized or valued presence, as described in this chapter, as a skill in my workplace.
2. I see where I could improve in this skill, and I don't normally do even what professionals do in this area. I try avoiding doing anything extra, and if I can get out early, I do.
3. The professional behaviors and errors best describe how I approach this skill.
4. I've recently started focusing on having an All-Star presence with my decisions and actions.
5. I've been doing these All-Star actions with my presence for at least three to five years.

The Closer – Bullpen Bullets

- ★ **Be Actively Present:** Engage fully in meetings by asking thoughtful questions and contributing ideas so your presence adds value and gets noticed.
- ★ **Show Up Beyond the 9-to-5:** Attend company events and networking opportunities outside normal hours to increase visibility and demonstrate commitment.
- ★ **Build Connection Through Courage:** Step out of your comfort zone to form authentic relationships with new people, expanding your network and professional impact.

2

PERSONAL APPEARANCE

My personal goal during this chapter is simple: *Don't sound cynical.* I am aware I am a Gen Xer where, growing up, hooded sweatshirts were worn at outdoor events when it was cold or at home when I was sick. Wearing them anywhere else back in the '80s was heresy (and still is, to some degree). So I will work hard to be as objective as possible with the commentary. Being sarcastic or cynical is an easy trap to fall into—especially when talking about something as seemingly surface-level as professional appearance. But here's the truth: One of the simplest ways to stand out at an All-Star level, yet astonishingly one that many professionals *refuse* to do—yes, I said "refuse" because this is about effort, not skill or one's God-given looks—is to level up your physical appearance.

Nowadays, your physical appearance is being recognized as a skill by all ages. I was caught off guard by my teenage son's peer complimenting me on my appearance in a Gen Z way. "Mr. Hamilton, that's a nice fit," she said.

I turned to my son, a huge smile on my face. He was mortified that I just procured Gen Z credit on my clothes, by someone using *their* terms, knowing he would hear about it all day. "Son, did you hear that? I have a good fit!" I couldn't resist.

If you are deep in Gen X or earlier and not up to speed with Z lingo, "fit" is not a term for physical wellness; I was being applauded on my outfit (fit for short). Our "fit" absolutely has a place in this book, because there's a chance you could miss the mark if you don't give it some attention. And if there's a chance you miss an easy opportunity to hit the All-Star mark, this chapter can help.

Most companies have a dress code. Right now, especially in standard corporate office environments, the prevailing culture leans toward "smart casual." That typically means a decent pair of jeans and a polo shirt for men, or something comparable for women—casual slacks, a long-sleeve shirt, or a nice sweater. It's polished, but not overly formal.

I imagine part of my perspective on this is shaped by how I was raised. When in church most Sundays growing up, slacks and a button-up shirt were the baseline. I'd wear a nice polo on the "casual" occasions, like Sunday or Wednesday nights. Jeans always felt a little out of place for the congregation I was in, and shorts weren't even a fleeting thought for entering a sanctuary. I think my ten-year-old self would have a full-blown heart attack walking into some of the churches I've seen lately. But honestly, I'm glad things have changed. The stigma around attire no longer dissuades people from stepping into the presence of God. And that's a win in my opinion.

Now, do I respect the individuals who still dress to the nines in their Sunday best? Absolutely. I compliment them when I see them. But I also celebrate the people who simply *show up* to worship. Because here's the thing: God is not human. Yes, His Son Jesus came in human form—let's be very clear about that—but God's love is unconditional. He receives us as we are. Humans, though? We judge by appearances. That's science. Dr. Ben C. Fletcher wrote, "We may think that fashion is just profligate indulgence and our sunny personality will eclipse our dull attire or detract from the soup stains on our anorak. Untrue. What we wear speaks volumes in just a few seconds. Dressing to impress really is worthwhile and could even be key to success."[4]

You don't have to like that—it's fair to feel a certain way about it—but if you're a professional in the workforce aiming for an All-Star level, you must reconcile with this reality: Most people will draw some conclusions about you based on what they *see*.

Let me give you an extreme example, and then we'll scale it back. Imagine you're at a relative's wedding. Everyone's dressed up—suits, dresses, designer brands. The bridesmaids and groomsmen are looking sharp. Then the groom walks out with the pastor . . . in faded jeans and a polo shirt. The bride, meanwhile, comes down the aisle in a stunning white gown.

What's your first reaction?

You're not thinking about the groom's *heart*. You're wondering, *What's going on here?* You immediately form opinions about what must have happened. You may believe that something must have happened to his planned wardrobe. But what if someone told you that it's what he wanted to wear. Now you are wondering why he would take this moment so casually. And why would the bride be okay with it or anyone else, for that matter. This may be an extreme scenario, but the mental process you're experiencing right now over what someone is wearing; guess what? That's universal; we'd all be wondering these things if we were hit with this scenario. Because our eyes are not initially satisfied with what we see, even in our mind's eye. Now let's bring it back to the boardroom.

Say you're scheduled to present to a group of interns—five or six of them. The dress code? Smart casual. You're already planning to wear jeans and a polo, but since you're presenting, you decide to throw on a sport coat. Adding a coat is an All-Star move, by the way. Good on you.

You walk into the room. Most of the interns are in smart casual attire—jeans and a nice shirt. One or two interns have leveled up a bit—in a fashionable "smart casual" dress and another in pressed slacks. And then there's one young man in faded Levi's with holes in the knees and a hoodie. Hood up over his head, almost covering his eyes.

---

[4] Ben C. Fletcher, "What Your Clothes Might Be Saying About You," April 20, 2013, PsychologyToday.com, https://www.psychologytoday.com/us/blog/do-something-different/201304/what-your-clothes-might-be-saying-about-you.

PERFORMANCE POINT

Which person in this room describes the way you typically appear to others?

ⓘ ERROR WARNING

Professionals are typically satisfied when they are meeting dress code because they always know there will be one person around them dressed more slovenly or not putting much stock in themselves. No disrespect to those professionals. I appreciate the dress code compliance more than you know. But you don't catch the eye like the two in this example that leveled up their appearance game. It's your choice.

Back to your interns and the training you are conducting. Be honest—your brain is forming opinions right now about the intern with the hoodie up and the casual jeans. You're making mental assessments without knowing anything about these individuals' work ethic, skills, or character. And that's the science! So why not *use* it to your advantage going forward?

If you're wondering what the benefits are to leveling up your appearance game, here's the short list:

- You'll stand out—without saying a word.
- People are naturally drawn to clean, well-put-together individuals. It's attraction in a professional, not romantic, sense.
- Executives notice—whether you're playing it safe or pushing into All-Star territory.
- Lastly, you gain benefit psychologically as well. Hutson and Rodriguez found measurable performance increased when professionals were better dressed.[5] A study from Temple University in the *Academy of Management Journal* showed that

[5] Matthew Hutson and Tori Rodriguez, "Dress for Success: How Clothes Influence Our Performance," January 1, 2016, ScientificAmerican.com, https://www.scientificamerican.com/article/dress-for-success-how-clothes-influence-our-performance/.

> daily clothing aesthetics and uniqueness had effects on self-esteem and downstream behavioral consequences.[6]

If you're the kind of professional who bends the dress code just a little—you know who you are—you might be wearing sneakers that *almost* pass for dress shoes, then acting surprised if anyone calls you out. Just know this: People see it. Executives see it. They know you're flirting with the bottom line—not shooting for the top.

On the other hand, All-Stars invest in their look. They're tuned in to current dress trends. They might spend a little extra on a wardrobe that sharpens their brand. And executives trust them for it. Those are the people execs don't worry about bringing into a high-stakes meeting, because they *know* they'll be dressed appropriately.

If you're only ever dressing to the baseline standard, here's the hard truth: You're already behind. Executives don't want to *have to* tell you what to wear. It reminds them of telling their third grader to put on socks that match. It's not about being fancy—it's about trust.

That being said, there's a valid fear of overdressing or misreading the room, and we'll get into that. But the takeaway here is this: All-stars know what each moment requires. Professionals don't always have that intuition, but it can be developed.

This is low-hanging fruit, and yet it's wildly valuable. Yes, you may need to skip your Starbucks for a couple of months and spend that $500 on new clothes. (And yes, do the math—six-dollar drinks every weekday add up fast.)

What's wild is how many professionals would rather be known for having that trendy green straw and plastic cup in hand than for being consistently sharp and All-Star ready. I hope the caramel latte is worth it.

Okay, maybe that's a little harsh, but I've got to be straight with you. Fewer and fewer leaders are willing to talk about appearance anymore. It's risky. For example, in some states, certain laws prevent leaders from saying anything about an employee's hairstyle. So if someone shows up

---

[6] Joseph K. Kim, Brian C. Holtz, and Ryan M. Vogel, "Wearing Your Worth at Work: The Consequences of Employees' Daily Clothing Choices," *Academy of Management Journal* 66, no. 5 (2023), https://doi.org/10.5465/amj.2021.1358.

rocking a full Billy Ray Cyrus mullet, it's not safe to mention it—even if it's not helping their physical appearance and brand.

That's why having mentors—trusted ones, preferably outside your organization—is crucial. These are people who will shoot straight about your appearance and help you level up.

No shade to the mullet, but if you're serious about climbing the ladder, scroll through LinkedIn profiles of executives in your industry. Check out the management team bios on the websites of companies you admire. Ask yourself, *What do I see?*

If your mindset is, "I'll be a trailblazer. If they don't promote me because of my look, so be it," I respect the courage. I admire the confidence. But I also want you to understand the *science* of it all. With all due respect to Billy Ray, that haircut isn't giving you the best odds of being seen as an All-Star.

ORANGE FLECKS

Let me give you a real story. One of my first executive board board dinners—this was a big moment. At end of the workday, I swing by my CFO's office. I'm wearing slacks, a sport coat, and a navy blue dress shirt with orange flecks. I thought it showed personality, and I specifically picked it out that morning for the event that evening.

He looks up and says, "That's some shirt you have there. I like the orange. You're going to change before the board dinner, right?"

PERFORMANCE POINT

Could you handle that kind of direct feedback about what you're wearing? What would your reaction be?

ⓘ ERROR WARNING

When I first read this experience out loud to a Generation Z coworker, they bristled and their jaw dropped. They couldn't believe my boss would say that to me. The instinct to take personal offense is there, and most professionals will go home and complain to their spouse or friend about what their boss dared to say to them. And these are good professionals, good at their job, who are taken aback. All-stars don't take offense; they change clothes. You've got to extend *implicit trust* to your leadership. If you believe they truly want the best for you, it's much easier to grow in your organization. Not every boss is an All-Star themselves, but the great majority of them do want you to win.

I hadn't planned to change at all; I thought I was spot-on with my choice in dress. That shirt was my *jam*. Looking back, my wife would have never let me out the door with it on either—but I'd left early that morning before she could approve the outfit. That CFO shot me straight because he *believed* in me. And I'm glad he said something, even though he made fun of that shirt for the next three months.

That was the moment it really sank in for me: Small stuff, such as shirt style, really does matter.

All-Star Action Tips

Let's close out this chapter with a few easy, actionable steps you can take to the office tomorrow:

1. Keep a jacket or coat handy.

At your desk, in your car, wherever. Men and woman both. Pick a jacket or coat that complements your style and keep it handy. One of our executives, who's known around our company for her fashion sense, always has a coat hanging in her office on standby—ready for pop-up meetings, client lunches, award ceremonies, you name it. She has a couple she rotates as standbys. I can assure you, though, she was fashionable long before becoming an executive. Don't wait for the promotion. Heed the cliché: "Dress for the job you desire."

2. Observe your executives.

Note their *brand*—their *style*. If your executives wear jeans and a polo or short-sleeve button-up shirt, take that as your baseline and go one level up. In this case, a polo with slacks or a sport coat over jeans shows you're ready if you need to step in.

3. Retire worn-out attire.

Shoes, belts, sweaters, jackets—people *see* the scuffs, the leather fading, and the belt falling apart, and either they are uncomfortable saying something, or they are just letting you be average alongside all the other professionals wearing the same loafer or slides three days a week.

4. Invite others to comment on your appearance.

If they know you are easy to approach about it, you will get feedback all the time.

5. Double-check what others are wearing if you're unsure.

This will help you catch those times where you are concerned about overdressing. Just verify with someone in the group if others will be in a suit and tie. Ironically, during the editing process of this book, I visited a chief human resources officer (CHRO) for a major publicly traded company in Houston, Texas, to discuss strategy. It was a Friday, and I had on jeans and a polo with my favorite Nike Dunks (we allow tennis shoes in my office on Fridays because they're optional work-from-home days). Before I left my house, I texted my CHRO colleague to verify the dress code at his company, and he texted back, "Business casual—I'm in khakis and a polo today." I changed clothes quickly before I went. Even though he's a great leader who would have welcomed me regardless, it would've been merely professional to assume jeans and a polo were fine—and never think to inquire. All-Stars will send the text, then change outfits if necessary.

Personal Appearance Self-Reflection

This self-evaluation is for *you*. If you want to share with a trusted peer or leader to build accountability toward your newly acquired skills, that is a bonus. At the very least, if you are choosing to make a run at being an All-Star, personal accountability can start here. Decide which number below applies most to you at this point and circle the number.

1. I've never recognized or valued personal appearance as a skill, as described in this chapter, in my workplace. I don't think it matters.
2. I see where I could improve in this skill, and I don't normally do what professionals do in this area. I slack in this.
3. The professional behaviors and "errors" best describe how I approach this skill. My personal appearance is currently up to standard.
4. I recently adopted the All-Star skills, behaviors, and actions. I'm better dressed and groomed better than most of my coworkers.
5. I've been doing these All-Star actions with my appearance for three to five years.

The Closer - Bullpen Bullets

- ★ **Audit and Upgrade Your Wardrobe:** Compare your daily work attire to what executives wear and make one or two simple upgrades to instantly elevate your professional appearance.
- ★ **Find a Style Mentor:** Seek honest feedback from a trusted All-Star outside your company to refine your appearance and gain an edge most people overlook.
- ★ **Dress for the Role You Want—Not the Role You Have:** Consistently plan your outfits to reflect the next level you're aiming for, signaling readiness and professionalism before you even speak.

3

RESOLVE

According to the *Oxford Dictionary,* the term *resolve* refers to "the firm determination to do something."

When I asked peers and mentors what they thought were the skills necessary to climb the corporate ladder and be an All-Star in an organization, specifically when it came to succeeding despite tough circumstances, I kept hearing trendy terms to describe this "it" factor for All-Star employees: "drive," "inner drive," "hunger," "determination," "ownership," and "grit," to name a few.

Harkening back to Coach Hadley Hicks (from the introduction) and his all-too-accurate assessment of how I often sought improved methods, none of those terms my peers provided seemed to satisfy what I was talking about. I believed there was a "better way" of describing the skill that seemed to reside in the soul of an All-Star and results in an undeterred approach to their vision of what is possible.

"It's bigger than that," I would respond to my colleagues. It's not something mysterious or immeasurable, because how do you really measure "hunger" outside of how many pieces of fried chicken someone can eat? (Sidebar: My father can eat anywhere from twelve to sixteen pieces of fried chicken, and he weighs 210 pounds. He's a legend in Hutchinson, Kansas. My in-laws from there still talk about "that one time we ate chicken together.")

This word needs to be something people can say they exemplified on a project or task that harbored challenges, foreseen or not. *Drive* or *determination* doesn't do it; everyone who ever worked with me or for me is going to claim they were determined or driven, and they were.

I have a weird fascination with listening to soundtracks of movies when I need a little extra motivation while working or writing. One of my favorites is the soundtrack to *National Treasure*. If you haven't seen this movie, put the book down, grab your kids (if you have them), and go back to the age of twelve with them for two hours. You won't regret it.

Without spoiling it for you, Ben Gates, the main character, clue decryptor and treasure hunter, described the Declaration of Independence as "ironclad" and "resolved." That was it. Resolve. The founding fathers had a firm determination to act, to accomplish, to improve, to change. Despite what movies or historical art may show you about the signing day of the Declaration, this was anything but a party and festive time for the signers. Pennsylvania's representative at the time, Benjamin Rush, described the moment as pensive and "an awful silence" when they signed the Declaration on August 2, 1776 (that's not a typo, July 4 was the approving of the final draft, not the signing). It was silent because they were putting their names on a treasonous document punishable by death. Not exactly a celebratory moment. Regardless, they all had resolve—a firm determination to do something. The signers were resolved to build a nation.

The word *resolve* did not find its way into the Declaration, but the determination to do something officially began with Richard Henry Lee's proposal to Congress on June 7, 1776. To propose a resolution on independence, the first provision Lee wrote went as follows: "Resolved, that these United Colonies are, and of right ought to be, free and independent states, that they are absolved from all allegiance to the

British Crown, and that all political connection between them and the state of Great Britain is, and ought to be, totally dissolved."[7]

Read into the etymology of the word *resolve* and we find it's a late Middle English word rooted in *solve*, as in to solve a problem, coming from the Latin *resolvere*, in which the "re" means "to express intensive force."

That's it—the use of intensive force to solve a problem. Resolve. When distributing these chapter topics and summaries to C-suite level individuals across the nation to see if the chapters of this book "covered it," one of my mentors said, "I like resolve; we call it grit." Another CEO, Shawn Patterson (whom you'll find in my acknowledgments), when I asked if something was missing, responded, "Passion may be missing, but that is probably the combination of presence and resolve."

Just a quick aside regarding Mr. Patterson's comment, and one easy to miss but so valuable. If you as the reader strive to develop these skills throughout all the chapters in this book, you will see they do not work independent of one another; they compound and complement one another and result in leaders in your company seeing you approach the day with a toolbox of skills. It may result in them describing you with more difficult terms to measure, such as *desire*, *persistence*, or, as Shawn Patterson would offer, *passion*.

Dr. Carol Dweck references this type of mental fortitude in her book *Mindset: The New Psychology of Success* where she coins the term *growth mindset:* "The passion for stretching yourself and sticking to it, even (or especially) when it's not going well, is the hallmark of the growth mindset. This is the mindset that allows people to thrive during some of the most challenging times in their lives."[8]

I contend resolve is a direct result of having a growth mindset.

High-ranking executives, especially CEOs, have resolve and use it time and again. They have to, because there is no one else to swoop in from above and solve the problems and make the decisions that need to be made. They are at "the end of the line." "The buck stops with them." Choose your cliché. A professional's ability (or lack thereof) to exercise

---

[7] "Lee Resolution (1776)," National Archives, Archives.gov, reviewed February 8, 2022, https://www.archives.gov/milestone-documents/lee-resolution.

[8] Carol S. Dweck, *Mindset: The New Psychology of Success: How We Can Learn to Fulfill Our Potential* (Ballantine Books, 2007), 7.

resolve is noticeable and measurable. Are they able to properly forecast, maneuver, and execute through the problems or challenges that are guaranteed to come, or do they cave to the circumstances and abdicate the problem-solving opportunity, claiming there's nothing else they can do when the proverbial kick in the teeth occurs?

Twice Gut-Punched

Such was the case when I was in an important, high-leverage recruiting season for a pipeline company. Initially, my Chief Administrative Officer (CAO) and I were delighted. (Delight often seems to precede unforeseen barriers to success.) In our desperate search to fill an executive role, we had two candidates who interviewed extremely well. Both indicated excitement for the opportunity and an affinity for our company. We felt either candidate would be extremely successful. As the search for the role was occurring in January, the CEO asked us our status so he could update the company during the annual company-wide business meeting that was occurring a few days later. The business meeting was held at our headquarters and broadcast to the six states in which we operated. This was a very well-known vacancy across the company, and many were eager to know about its filling, especially the CEO. We communicated to the CEO we were definite it would be by the end of the quarter, if not the end of the month. I had a feeling it was going to be by the end of the month in my discussions with the candidates; the quarter end, eleven weeks away, seemed an overly conservative estimate. Our main job now was deciding which one to offer first; they were neck and neck, very strong candidates. We decided and sent the offer to our first choice.

PERFORMANCE POINT

When a project or initiative is going exactly how you envisioned, do you enjoy the ride, or are you working your backup plan? Spoiler alert, the chapter title somewhat gives away what will happen here, so the performance point is key.

ⓘ ERROR WARNING

How many times have you heard "That won't happen"? It sunk the Titanic. Time is precious, and this doesn't mean you should have your entire Plan B complete and operable to the letter if Plan A is going just as planned, but All-Star performers have Plan B in place where it can be up and running in short order. Professionals trust when Plan A is going smooth, there is no reason to spend time working Plan B.

"Our search is going well and our candidates are promising, so I'm happy to say we'll have our division leader in place by the end of the quarter," the CEO communicated during the company-wide update to the better part of five hundred employees.

Being included in any part of the company update was a moment of pride. It didn't matter if my name was mentioned; I was just proud I was directly working on something the CEO thought was critical enough to announce to the entire company. The dreamer in me was hoping I'd have the signed offer right before the CEO took to the podium so he could announce it then and there like a breaking news update, but that stayed a dream.

The results were nothing short of a nightmare. But as mentioned earlier, resolve entails solving a problem, and a problem quickly emerged from what seemed like a very seamless executive search.

I received the first decline from our top candidate the evening after the CEO made his announcement; that one hurt. The second candidate had just completed his interview days prior, so the offer to him wasn't delayed enough for him to find another opportunity elsewhere or discourage him from signing, so we were optimistic he would accept. But that candidate declined a couple of days later as well. Now the nausea set in. We had no more offers to make.

The deadline of the end of the quarter, just promised to the entire company, now seemed like it was fastly approaching, and I felt I had put the CEO's word in jeopardy. We had a little over ten weeks to source candidates, interview, offer, sign, potentially relocate, and onboard an executive.

PERFORMANCE POINT

What was the order of action when you had your most recent difficult or seemingly impossible challenge or problem with a project or deadline? Did you just figure it was impossible and say, "We can't make that happen," and give up on the change or improvement plan, or did you miss a deadline but have a "justifiable reason"? Did you call your boss and ask, "What do we do now?"

ⓘ ERROR WARNING

Here's where professionals and All-Stars are separated by resolve quickly. Many people call moments like these a "kick in the teeth" or "punch in the gut." What you had finished, wrapped up, or made a done deal ended with anything but, and you feel all the work was for naught and in some cases you are physically sick. Many of you have felt this. Still, what was your answer to the above performance point? If you threw your hands in the air and moved the deadline, went back to the old way, or immediately called your boss without considering options for what to do next, this is a common *professional* move. And it's okay and very reasonable. This was an unforeseen and rare circumstance to have both interested candidates decline. Feeling out of options or stuck is normal. It's frankly hard to call this an error if you tend to stop in these types of circumstances, but you're wanting to be an All-Star, not just another professional. All-stars handle this differently. They have resolve—the ability to use intensive force to solve a problem.

I would be remiss, given my Houston, Texas, upbringing, if I didn't reference the late Jim Lovell, astronaut of the Apollo 13 mission to the moon. While many remember the "Houston, we have a problem" quote that began the harrowing ordeal in front of that crew, Lovell and the crew's resolve was literally lifesaving. This is also evident in Lovell's view of complex problems, which captures the heart of his resolve, for he once said, "Be thankful for problems. If they were less difficult, someone with less ability might have your job."

And we had a problem, a recruiting problem. I still remember feeling nauseous dialing the next candidate on my list the same evening our second offer decline happened. Read that carefully: the *same* evening. But at least I had candidates to call! Remember Plan B? We had been building this backup list even during the interviewing process of our first set of candidates we thought were sure shots. That was Plan B—continue to source the position and have at least ten viable candidates to call if something crazy happens. Well, crazy happened. Had we not built Plan B, I may have passed out and likely never written this chapter or this book.

Within days of round two of vetting, hours of phone assessments, conversations, and whittling down candidates, I had four candidates who were solid semifinalists. There was another slight challenge, though. In our first round of assessments to select our finalists to bring to headquarters, my CAO and I had flown to the location of the semifinalists to meet them, making it easier on their schedules. In that first round, they were all from the same general area, so we only had to fly to one city.

Doing this would take much more time in this second round of vetting as our semifinalists were from different states, nowhere near each other. Adopting our round 1 strategy would push the Q1 commitment too far out. Working with four candidates' schedules against my CAO's was an enormous challenge; this wasn't going to work as it had before.

I offered a plan to the CAO that would cut down on time and give us a better chance to stay on track in filling the role. He agreed that we should give it a shot.

It worked. Somehow, all the semifinalists agreed to having us fly them into a major airport only a two-hour drive away from my CAO and I. The candidates would stay overnight in an airport hotel and fly back the next day after their respective interviews. This allowed my CAO to spend only two nights away and a moderate drive from the office and accomplish the same task as we had in round 1.

My CAO cleared his schedule, and we flew four candidates in and interviewed them across two days in the hotel restaurant, one in the morning, one at night so the candidates didn't cross paths. My CAO and I had memorized the hotel restaurant menu by the time we left.

More importantly, we were elated to find two great finalists from the four. We brought them to headquarters two weeks later to go through the same interviewing process with other executives. A worthy candidate rose to the top. We had another offer out less than a month after the CEO announcement to the company. While extremely fatigued, the CAO and I were, in hindsight, somewhat relieved that the first two had declined, because our most recently chosen candidate checked even more boxes for what the company needed. We had renewed high hopes with the offered candidate.

Days later the offer was accepted! There are not many times I've cheered or fist-pumped in a corporate role similar to when my baseball players in my coaching days hit a game-winning home run or one of my pitchers struck the last guy out with the winning run stranded on base. But I hooped and hollered when that signed offer came through.

Now the next "problem:" get this executive in the door in less than eight weeks, fulfilling the "end of the quarter" commitment made by my CEO to the company. For those unfamiliar with recruiting executives, it's important to note that executives at this level typically give a minimum of thirty days' notice, not two weeks, to the employer they are leaving (after the new company's background check clears). Then they often go on a vacation before starting the new job. I am unsure if anyone in our company would have cared or noticed if the executive started a week or two after the end of the quarter. But I did. The CEO, because of my guidance, had said, "By the end of the quarter."

PERFORMANCE POINT

When you've worked a project through a major challenge and the accomplishment outweighs the importance of minor details at the end, do you feel justified in disregarding those smaller details?

ⓘ ERROR WARNING

Professionals who are reliable complete work and accomplish difficult tasks in a reasonable amount of time, often in or around the time necessary to consider it a job well done. If you want to be an All-Star, it is an error to have a mindset of "reasonable," "around," or "ish" associated with your ability to get something done. While for many projects or jobs it may be good enough, you will have a hard time being seen as an All-Star who can overcome obstacles and challenges and still get to the finish line on time and on budget. Finish strong, finish as you committed, regardless of the major unforeseen hurdle you navigated.

As our new executive was working through exiting his current company and beginning relocation logistics, he and I discussed the Q1 commitment the CEO had made to the workforce, and he was gracious enough to do the best he could to make it happen. Though rushed and showing his own resolve, he thought midweek in the first week of April would be best to onboard. This was reasonable and just days after the end of the quarter. He was wanting to settle his family into their new home before starting at the office.

"Will you be driving up that preceding weekend?" I asked.

"Yes, we'll start heading up on Saturday, the thirty-first, and try to get about halfway," he answered.

I asserted, "Then we'll make your official start date March 31 since you are beginning the relocation as a condition of the employment agreement. Then we'll begin the onboarding later that week." And with that, we satisfied the commitment the CEO had made to the company.

PERFORMANCE POINT

When you accomplish a complex task or project amid unforeseen obstacles and challenges, is your first reaction to advertise what you did and what was up against you?

ⓘ ERROR WARNING

I'll yield to an excellent saying regarding seeking kudos for your big wins requiring resolve (and we'll talk about Gratitude later) to a corporate peer of mine, Tracy Dieterich. He offered me a great saying that captures executives' mentalities about these accomplishments: "They don't want to hear about the storms; they just want to know if the ship came in." Don't let this discourage you on your journey to All-Star. Executives know if you are achieving big goals, you are showing resolve. They don't need to hear about the storms; they've been through them and know they are there. It's an All-Star move not to talk about the storms—until you write about them (wink emoji).

Only four people, the CAO, myself and our wives, really knew the circumstances and setbacks to get that project across the finish line. The CEO never knew the organized chaos and long nights it took to make the deadline; probably until now.

Later that year after landing the executive, when commenting on the executive hire accomplishment in a performance review, my CAO described my effort as showing "doggedness." I actually considered that word among the other words for this chapter and performance criteria, but it likely required a deeper explanation than *resolve*, and it wasn't as cool because it didn't appear in the movie *National Treasure*.

Not just having been through challenges where resolve was required to succeed, I have had the pleasure to see it firsthand by many people I surround myself with. And I believe observing it is key to being able to exercise it myself. Following are three such cases of people demonstrating All-Star resolve at work.

1. My wife has an incredible resolve in her photography when she takes someone's photos. She's an artist, and she refuses to put her name on something that doesn't pass her keen eye. It's not uncommon for her to scout out locations around town because she refuses cookie-cutter backdrops; she wants her clients to have backdrops that no one has ever seen. If you are near her when she is either taking photos or editing them, she looks for things no one else looks for and sees things no one else can see. She's had

opportunities to outsource editing, but when a picture doesn't turn out the way she envisioned, she digs in with hours of editing, showing the resolve in making sure the final product exceeds her high artistic bar. She'll try to explain how certain lines and shapes work against the shadows and point out jaw lines and other cool-sounding words like that. I can only say things like, "I like the big tree in the picture." She also works tirelessly in making sure clients enjoy getting their photos taken. Can you imagine actually enjoying getting photos taken? Her clients do. She uses intensive force to figure out a way to make the process a delight for every client; she shows resolve.

2. The managing partner of the public accounting firm I work for faced a multimillion-dollar ransomware attack, three weeks before the April 15 IRS deadline. Countless clients' tax returns were now at risk. The fastest route would have been to pay the ransom and, if we were lucky enough, not go out of business. If we would have done that, we'd have frozen hiring, likely cut jobs, frozen raises, eliminated bonuses, tightened spending, raised rates, and risked losing clients. Additionally, he learned that even after receiving an exorbitant ransom, these cyber criminals often do not grant all the access back. But he has resolve. He found a way to invest a fraction of the ransom amount the hackers were asking for, instead of paying the ransom, and do the hard work of building back the firm's IT and security infrastructure. This required finding outsourced experts in the cybersecurity field to essentially take up residence in our offices and remedy the hack. Then our managing partner, the cyber security team, and our internal IT team took up an entire office floor and worked eighteen to twenty hours a day for the next week building an assembly line to wipe almost every laptop in the company from four cities and research the entire network to find the holes where the criminals entered our network. Additionally, there were countless hours spent re-creating files and documents over the course of the next several months. Because of the resolve of the managing partner, the firm served our clients on

time, didn't miss a year of raises, didn't see hiring slow down, and even paid bonuses one month after the attack.

3. Back when I was a collegiate baseball coach, an assistant coach I was very familiar with had left the world of college baseball. As a baseball coach at that level, you know that if you leave the game to take a job not associated with college baseball, it is very difficult to get back into the college level. I had admired his talent over the years, and while speaking with him over the phone, he told me he was substitute teaching sixty miles away from where I was coaching. He was waiting for a full-time high school teaching job to open up; the college game wasn't working out for him. I told him, "I don't have any money because it's committed, but if you want to stay in the game, I'll find the uniform and you can be my pitching coach." Although I couldn't even scrounge up money to help with gas, he still drove sixty miles one way every day in a beat-up sedan we could hear sputtering from a mile away. Subsequently, he built the best pitching staff I ever had on a team over the course of the next season. That's resolve. And it's part of why he succeeded me as head coach the next year, won a conference championship, then moved on to a bigger school just three years later and has won two national championships and two national Coach of the Year awards. As I write this book, he is now a pitching coach at the NCAA division 1 level after having spent a year coaching for the New York Yankees organization—this is the residue of great resolve.

These are All-Stars when it comes to resolve. It's easy to measure, easy to calculate. Whether it's tirelessly editing to fine-tune shadows in photographs, beating cyber attackers at their own game, or resurrecting a college coaching career, it's easy to see how they all have used intensive force to solve problems.

When individuals build a career with this type of resolve, year after year, their performances are at the Hall of Fame level, up there near where John Hancock and his comrades became "resolved."

There are excellent professionals, consistent at their jobs, who don't exercise resolve. Challenges and problems happen, and professionals will get through them, but often by taking the cues and resting on the strength and courage of their superiors, who understand the circumstances "no one saw coming." Employees who are still developing may quit, blame someone, or may never be given the projects in the first place. Many professionals may outperform those who are still developing, but professionals still settle for the easier or less strenuous path. That's natural. But it's not showing resolve, either by choice or ignorance. Choosing the easier path is not "bad," but it does limit the chances of professionals from becoming All-Stars in their organization.

Exercise resolve. Be an All-Star. Fly up your organization.

Resolve Self-Reflection

This self-evaluation is for *you*. If you want to share with a trusted peer or leader to build accountability toward your newly acquired skills, that is a bonus. At the very least, if you are choosing to make a run at being an All-Star, personal accountability can start here. Decide which number below applies most to you at this point and circle the number.

1. I avoid challenges or barriers and have considered quitting when it comes to my work. I feel it's not my job to solve problems.
2. I see where I could improve in this skill, because I typically freeze or worry when an unforeseen challenge happens where I can't think about solutions.
3. The professional behaviors and "errors" best describe how I approach this skill. I'm a solid employee in the midst of challenges and can often offer sound suggestions.
4. I've had opportunities and experiences similar to ones described in this chapter where I've been a key person others turn to for answers and action in the face of challenge.
5. I've had to exercise resolve and have had success over numerous challenges for at least three to five years.

The Closer – Bullpen Bullets

- ★ **Build a "Plan B" Before You Need It:** Always have a backup strategy ready so you can keep moving forward when obstacles appear.
- ★ **Practice Finishing Exactly as Promised:** Follow through on every commitment exactly as planned to strengthen your reliability and credibility.
- ★ **Reframe Problems as Opportunities to Prove Your Capability:** Treat every setback as a chance to demonstrate your resolve, creativity, and leadership.

4

RELATIONSHIPS

Let me share the point of this chapter right up front: You must build and cultivate genuine relationships to achieve the pinnacle of your career.

The day I started writing this chapter, it happened to be the first full post–COVID-19 pandemic day: May 13, 2023. The national public health emergency had been officially lifted. A historic day.

What does that have to do with relationships?

Everything.

From March 2020 to May 2023, we experienced one of the most significant litmus tests of whether relationships—specifically, in-person ones—are a critical factor in the success of both companies and individuals.

On March 16, 2020, at ten a.m., I sat in the corner suite of our managing partner's office with members of the executive committee. That was the moment we made the call: Send everyone home and work remotely until we could make sense of the phenomenon of COVID that had just shaken the world.

From that day forward, companies and communities all responded in their own ways to navigate the pandemic and try to stay in business. Some succeeded. Some failed.

Our firm? Likely one of the most progressive and successful in how we navigated the entire journey.

Our workforce, by the government's standard, was defined as "essential." That word hits different now than it did before that time. For those who don't remember, if you were defined "essential," the patchwork of interpreting rules from local politicians about whether or not you could report to work didn't apply. The decision was ours as a company—not a county judge's or a state official's.

By July 2020, only five months after initially sending employees home, our executives made what was considered at the time a bold move: a return to the office three days a week. You saw that right; five months after the world shut down, we came back to the office, and we had no restrictions, no sitting in every other chair, no arrows on the floor for walking directions, or distinguishing entrances from exits. It would be a year until that decision would be adopted by the majority of companies across the nation.

Ask our executives why they brought workers back so soon, and you'll hear something simple yet profound: The risk of losing our culture—driven by our open, relational environment—was in the balance. Before you assume we were draconian, we did tell our workforce that if they fell into the chronic health condition population that was at the most risk, they should stay home. And I even personally told some they shouldn't come in even though they desired to do so. The majority of our workforce, however, was younger corporate accounting professionals who normally kept professional "distance." No one worked in tight quarters or shoulder to shoulder on an assembly line. The COVID-19 numbers and statistics that some of our best auditors researched showed a very low risk for office transmission in our line of work.

Regardless, our executives' call to bring employees back to the office in July of 2020 was an incredible decision. But it proved to be the right one. During the year in which we tracked COVID as a company, there were no office transmissions.

Years later, those same executives would be on calls guiding other companies on how to get their people back into the office. Why? Because the working world had rediscovered something fundamental: Relationships drive success. And they also needed people back in the office, but getting them back in after eighteen months of "work from home" was a heavy lift.

In May 2023, bumper-to-bumper traffic during my commute had returned. My twenty-six-mile, thirty-minute "COVID" drive to downtown Houston? Now it was back to an hour. Both ways.

Why?

Relationships.

In a keynote speech I often give, I recount conversations I've had with C-suite executives I've worked alongside—or directly for—when I asked them what behaviors I exhibited that led them to trust me with promotion-level responsibilities and a seat at their table.

I thought they'd say it was my energy, my charisma, or my positivity.

They didn't.

They said it was the relationships I cultivated—in the office. Both formal ones and, more importantly, informal ones.

A chief operations officer once said during one of these individual surveys, "You had the eyes and ears of the workforce, keeping the C-suites grounded."

PERFORMANCE POINT

What relationships have you cultivated with people in your office?

Who do you know in other departments or divisions?

Have you had lunch with individuals in various roles—both above and below your level?

Do you know anything about their families, hobbies, or interests?

ⓘ ERROR WARNING

If your honest answer to most of those questions is "none" or "no," then your promotional ceiling is severely limited. Failure to build relationships in your company is what we call a "career-limiting move."

Of all the potential errors in this book, I'd rate this one in the top three.

If you're still holding this book but would really like to toss it across the room right now, it's probably because someone saying that your career climb is based on the types of relationships you create versus your talent alone hits a nerve.

Maybe you're technically elite—one of the best in your division or department—and you just don't have those kinds of relationships. Let's be clear: Your value to your company is undeniable. Technical skill is hard to find, and if you've got it, that alone is commendable. It's . . . professional.

But if you're looking to grow professionally and can't figure out why your advancement has stalled, and you want to be an All-Star in your company, this could very well be your ceiling.

Keith Ferrazzi, in his book, *Never Eat Alone*, referenced this exact approach saying, "Independent people who do not have the skills to think and act interdependently may be good individual producers, but they won't be seen as good leaders or team players. Their careers will begin to stutter and stall before too long."[9]

And while it's tough to label this a "mistake," because building relationships isn't easy, the good news is this: It's fixable. So let's fix it.

Alicia

There was an accounting employee I used to visit who I'm convinced was one of the best grandmothers in the world. She adored taking her grandkids on vacation—and loved telling me all about it. Disney was always a highlight. We'd laugh about how anyone who goes to Disney probably needs a vacation *after* Disney.

[9] Keith Ferrazzi, *Never Eat Alone: And Other Secrets to Success, One Relationship at a Time* (Crown Currency, 2014), 17.

Her name was Alicia. She was a bright spot in the company—always smiling, always helpful, always asking how my family was doing, and always quick to share how hers was. I didn't work in accounting. My office wasn't even remotely close to that department.

But I dropped in anyway.

I made it a habit to drop in to as many offices and cubes as I could. Not long visits—just micro check-ins. I'd open with "Hey, how are you?" and, based on the response, determine if there was an opportunity to ask more.

Why?

Because getting to know the people you work with gives you insight into how they think, how they feel, and what really makes the company tick.

More than that, it made work enjoyable.

PERFORMANCE POINT

What types of non-work-related questions do you ask fellow employees—open-ended or one-word-answer questions?

ⓘ ERROR WARNING

Professionals are typically very cordial, offering a "hello" and "how are you?" Those are fifteen-second and surface-level discussions only. Not All-Star. All-stars offer open-ended conversations (e.g., "Tell me how Disney with the grandkids went!").

Think about why we love being with certain friends or family. It's because we *know* them and feel known by them. So why not invest just a little time to "know" the people in your company in a similar way?

You don't need ten minutes at every stop. Two minutes. Just two minutes.

Before you say, "I don't have time," consider this: Five two-minute check-ins a day equals ten minutes. That's probably less time than you spend scrolling social media at your desk

(Gotcha!)

If you do that every workday, you'll complete around sixty check-ins a month—even if you're in a hybrid office reporting model. After six months, you'll have had three or four interactions with most of your coworkers. You'll know birthdays, anniversaries, vacation stories, maybe even who has recently lost loved ones.

For just ten minutes a day.

Now, imagine a leadership position opens up. Who do you think stands out more—the highly technical employee no one really knows or the somewhat technical employee who also has a reputation for checking in with people, remembering names, and sending a card when someone's going through a tough time?

Executives notice. And yes, they ask around.

They want someone who can *rally* a workforce or show support for others, not just someone who can complete a spreadsheet.

And for what it's worth, Alicia always gave me grace on the expense report deadline when I needed it.

I like to think it was because I asked about Disney.

But knowing Alicia? She's just that gracious.

ⓘ ERROR WARNING

This part is critical, and there is no performance point needed to bring this error up. If you try to use this strategy *just* to get promoted, it will fail. You must pursue relationships because we are humans and we work better socially.

The COVID pandemic proved the aforementioned error.

If your *primary* intent is to build relationships for personal gain, that's not relationship building. That's manipulation, where your intent is only to build others' confidence in you so you receive what you want. That's where the term "confidence man," better known as "con man," comes from.

Before you assume I'm preaching this lesson because I'm so great at it, let me admit something.

Relationship Fail

Remember my departure from college baseball coaching? That stemmed mostly from my *failure* to build genuine relationships. It's tough to admit, but looking back, I can see where I kept things transactional—or skipped the relationship-building part altogether. That approach capped my coaching career.

College athletics mirrors corporate America in a glaring way: Coaches and athletic directors tend to trust those they've *built* relationships with. It's often called the "coaching fraternity."

In corporate America, it's not much different.

Some might call that bias—and yes, there's some of that out there. But in most cases, promotional decisions or key external hires are made through genuine, trusted relationships.

I saw this time and again. Coaches who were let go would be back in the game almost immediately—usually on a staff where they had a strong, trusted relationship with someone. Or they got hired by an AD they'd had a previous connection with.

I figured my track record—turning two losing programs into winners—would be enough. When I "left" my second college (yes, those quotation marks are doing some heavy lifting for what truly happened), I didn't get any calls.

Worse? I had no one *to* call.

PAST PERFORMANCE POINT

If you've ever been laid off, let go, fired, or forced to make a change, did you have someone in your network to call—someone who could either help you navigate next steps or actually get you on board with their team?

If you haven't been in that spot yet, ask yourself who's in your phone right now whom you'd trust to help you land safely if you were let go.

ⓘ ERROR WARNING

Assuming you'll never be in that spot is a huge mistake, and many professionals make it.

All-star employees always have two to three people in their network they can call who would have the ability—and willingness—to help them find their next opportunity, if not create a spot on their team immediately.

During all those baseball conventions, tournaments, and recruiting weekends, I never built genuine relationships. Not the kind where I could call someone and say, "Hey, I need help."

I wasn't mean or cold. I was pleasant and respectful. But I wasn't *invested* or *curious*.

As a result, my coaching career ended—quietly.

Luckily, through the grace of God, support from loved ones, and some honest self-reflection, I realized my shortcoming.

So I changed.

I started valuing people for who they were—not what they could do for me.

It didn't happen overnight. It's not a light switch.

And if you've taken personality assessments, by looking at the following results of my scores: "E" for extroverted in Myers–Briggs; "i" for influence in DiSC; 7 on the Enneagram; and the "Entertainer" in 16 Personalities, you'd probably assume I'm naturally good at building relationships.

A "people person," right?

But here's the truth: Just because you can make someone smile doesn't mean you're building a relationship.

Spend those ten minutes a day *not* on yourself but investing in *others*.

Open doors. Open your career. Open your life.

Become more than an All-Star employee.

Become an All-Star human.

Ninety Seconds

After experiencing the reality of my coaching career being negatively affected in part by my transactional posture toward building relationships, I began to be intentional in improving this skill. The opportunities would come quickly as I began to seek out my next career move.

Toward the end of an intense eight-person panel interview for a position in an industry I knew little about, I locked eyes with Denis, an experienced engineer and leader.

I could tell Denis wasn't sold on me. Even I knew I was a bit of a fish out of water with this group of highly technical and educated professionals listening to how I connected my work experience with their employment needs.

Denis quipped back at me, saying, "This is not a training position. You need to know what you're doing. I'm going to ask you a question, and I'm giving you ninety seconds to finish the answer."

(Definitely the "bad cop" tactic.)

He continued, "A line explosion happens in the middle of the night. What do you do? Your ninety seconds start now . . . Go!"

After about five seconds, I answered, "Call my manager, drive to the location, and do whatever it is you're going to teach me to do." All the while, I hoped my attempts to hide the lump in my throat were successful.

At the end of the interview, they asked me if I had any questions. I always have questions, but I was so curious to know how well they thought I'd answered Denis' question, and I had to find out. And then I decided to approach it boldly.

I led off with, "Denis, same question you asked me. You've got ninety seconds . . . Go!"

He cracked a grin, stared me down for a second, and said, "The exact same thing you said."

I had won him over. And I breathed a huge sigh of relief.

We ended up working together for two years, always laughing about that interview. Denis eventually left for another energy company in Houston, where I grew up, but even to this day, we stay in touch.

Shortly after he left the Kentucky-based company he'd interviewed me for, he was diagnosed with cancer.

I put his name into my prayer app on my phone (the app is called Prayer NB, if you're interested). I set monthly reminders to check in. Missed some but mostly stayed consistent. We even met for coffee once in Houston when I was visiting family. I had coffee. Denis had tea. "Extra hot," he always says as he orders—which probably confuses the baristas. It confuses me.

PERFORMANCE POINT

Have you maintained contact with professional relationships after someone leaves your team or company?

ⓘ ERROR WARNING

Most professionals don't. But if you want to grow past just being a professional into something more, this is a must. All-stars don't just build relationships in their companies; they sustain them beyond the walls and for many years.

Three years after Denis left the company, he contacted me about an executive-level HR role at the company he was now an engineer for, a huge publicly traded energy company in downtown Houston.

I hadn't been planning a move to Houston. My wife, a Kansas native, was firmly against the idea—she loves seasons, snow, and winter, and Houston has none of them. (Sorry, Houstonians, but you know it's true).

But Denis's call prompted a serious discussion between us. Given some personal challenges we'd faced that year, maybe it *was* time to get closer to family.

Denis put in a good word with the CHRO.

I didn't end up at his company—but eight months later, I accepted a leadership role in HR in downtown Houston when others found out I was "on the market."

So Houston it was, as the next stop. Doing what I love.

And I believe—wholeheartedly—I wouldn't be here without Denis.

This is a decision point.

You have to decide whether you're content maintaining professional, surface-level relationships—or whether it's time to *high-grade* your connections.

Whether you want to just perform well at your job—or become an All-Star who leverages the power of meaningful relationships to launch your career to the highest level.

The choice is yours.

Relationships Self-Reflection

This self-evaluation is for *you*. If you want to share with a trusted peer or leader to build accountability toward your newly acquired skills, that is a bonus. At the very least, if you are choosing to make a run at being an All-Star, personal accountability can start here. Decide which number below applies most to you at this point and circle the number.

1. If I could do my job and never interact with people, I would prefer that.
2. I see where I could improve in this skill. I generally enjoy interaction, but I seldom try to connect with anyone in my place of employment.
3. The professional behaviors and "errors" best describe how I approach this skill. I've built what seem to be some decent connections, but if I am honest with myself, some of them are more transactional instead of genuine.
4. I've had relationship experiences similar to ones described in this chapter, where I know the value of those around me and engage with them in meaningful ways.
5. I've been building these types of genuine relationships for at least three to five years.

The Closer - Bullpen Bullets

- ★ **Invest Ten Minutes a Day in Genuine Connection:** Spend just a few minutes each day having real, open-ended conversations with coworkers to build trust and visibility beyond surface-level interactions.
- ★ **Strengthen and Sustain Your Network:** Regularly check in with former colleagues and mentors—even after they've left your company—to maintain relationships that could lead to future opportunities.
- ★ **Build Relationships Before You Need Them:** Cultivate authentic connections across departments now, so when change or challenges come, you have trusted allies ready to support your next move.

5

GRATITUDE

An executive mentor of mine has a great metaphor for gratitude. "You have to operate the curtains so people you work with can be recognized on the stage as much as possible. You can't worry about the fact that the crowd doesn't see you or applaud you; that's not the point."

Our culture, here in the first quarter of the twenty-first century, is having a hard time holding onto this skill. But it is a career and life limiter if you don't grasp the concept of gratitude and make it a part of your being.

I admit, this is an area I try to improve in often.

Social media has likes, follows, and subscribers; online reviews have stars; and now our companies have so many different methods and trendy versions to show employee appreciation. Seldom does a day go by that there is not some sort of group appreciation day. I discovered just days ago there was a "Human Resources Appreciation Day." It must happen on weekends because I've never received a card in my career.

Our culture is becoming intensely focused on how much appreciation they receive.

As an HR executive, I am often confronted by employees who explain their frustrations about not being appreciated for what they do. This is a very real challenge, and I remind leaders they really need to take a moment and give some accolades and shout-outs when they can; it makes a difference. That being said, professionals from whom I hear this complaint often pause when I ask them one question in return: "Have you communicated an appreciation for anything they've done for you?"

PERFORMANCE POINT

In times when you've felt underappreciated, have you immediately communicated to someone else that your boss or the company does not appreciate you?

ⓘ ERROR WARNING

Professionals often comment about feeling some degree of lack of appreciation for what they do. Again, fair, and this isn't to discredit those claims. The error here comes if there hasn't first been an introspective, honest reflection of the gratitude they have shown others.

Before reading on, please take note: I am not a CEO or president. I've gone from individual contributor to executive in a relatively short period of time. I know multiple CEOs, and I know how the good one's tick. Are there bad CEOs? Probably. Are they rare? Yes. But they can't get to that level and stay if they're bad. And there is a very good chance you have a good CEO. Go with the averages, and don't get offended by what you're about to read.

This is actually simple. Gratitude increases your engagement in your day-to-day life and work. High-level executives know this and execute on it. The reason is simple. On average, how many thank-you cards or moments of recognition do typical CEOs get from their employees? This is where the CEO reading this book is probably asking, "There are CEOs who get thank-you cards from employees?" I would be willing to bet a paycheck that most CEOs dish out at least four times as many words of recognition, affirmation, or thankfulness than they ever receive from the hundreds or thousands of employees those CEOs work tirelessly to keep employed. The disgruntled professional is scoffing at the last sentence or has stopped reading altogether and will likely remain a professional. No gratitude.

It is common to see engagement surveys where the employees at higher levels in the organization are typically more engaged and feel like they are a part of something meaningful. Skeptics will say "money" is the factor.

Gratitude Science

In studying engagement surveys, I discovered that those who make it a point to offer documented public recognition to others feel far more engaged and answer more positively to the specific statement "I feel I am a part of something meaningful" than those individuals who do not offer public recognition. Read that again. Yes, people who received public recognition but never gave any polled lower than those who gave public recognition.[10]

Recent research validates that giving recognition fosters deeper connections for the giver. The American Psychological Association has found that individuals who frequently express appreciation report higher job satisfaction and personal fulfillment. Acknowledging others reinforces the giver's role in creating a positive, collaborative work environment.[11]

In three recent surveys from my company, we were able to see aggregate engagement survey data from employees who gave public recognition in a formal system. Many companies have various software programs that allow tracking of senders and receivers of appreciation,

---

[10] Emily Martin and Jared Hamilton, "The Secret Sauce to Engaged Employees," Calvetti Ferguson, accessed September 29, 2025, https://calvettiferguson.com/engaged-employees/.

[11] "The Power of Gratitude in the Workplace," *American Psychological Association*, accessed September 15, 2025, https://www.psychologytoday.com/us/blog/radical-sabbatical/202009/the-power-of-gratitude-in-the-workplace.

so tracking is pretty simple. Most companies pay most attention to who did (or didn't) receive recognition or appreciation. Our company, additionally, focused on those who expressed appreciation in this way, exercising gratitude. Then we took that population and had the survey group calculate the aggregate sentiments on a specific statement that read, "I feel like I am a part of something meaningful."

The employee survey data studied over three years show that 95.7 percent of employees who gave recognition agreed with the statement about job meaningfulness. Of the population that did not give formal recognition, only 81 percent agreed that their job made them feel part of something meaningful.

This gap widened in the third year. Every employee who gave recognition felt like they were a part of something meaningful, compared to 79 percent of those who didn't provide formal recognition.

I also spoke with a similar-sized company that reported an 88 percent favorable response rate to the meaningfulness question. While they had a formal recognition system, they did not track who gave or didn't give recognition, so a direct comparison was difficult. Some companies that participated in the same survey and showed lower engagement results reported they had no formal recognition system at all.

Job meaningfulness was highlighted in a talent survey done by Deloitte as one of the top three drivers of employee engagement—a key aspect of retention.[12]

So if you are beginning to feel unappreciated, start recognizing and acknowledging the great people you work with, and call me in the morning and tell me how it makes you feel.

Bill

Bill was the head of a manufacturing division for Compaq computers, a large, publicly traded computer company in the early 1980s and through the early 1990s. He was brought over in 1984 to run the division because of his reputation for running plants and assembly lines for similar companies. Those who saw Bill in his building among all the

[12] "Become Irresistible: a new model for employee engagement," Deloitte.com, 2015, https://www.deloitte.com/us/en/insights/topics/talent/employee-engagement-strategies.html.

assembly lines say he never started or ended his day in his executive office upstairs, where the supervisor and manager offices were and where most of the managers liked to stay.

PERFORMANCE POINT

If you are a professional, would you rather send a text, MS Teams message, or email rather than get out of your cubicle to go deliver a message to someone? If you are a first-level supervisor or middle manager, do you crave being in your office?

ⓘ ERROR WARNING

Gratitude is extremely hard to convey as genuine without a personal visit. Even a thank-you card can be a personal visit when you choose to deliver it, when the intention is there. Professionals are quick to give a thumbs-up or the good ole "appreciate everything you do" in a chat or email. This is not gratitude. The All-Star is seeking to celebrate others in a personal way.

Bill would often be seen walking the assembly line talking to the workers. Sometimes about their challenges on the line, but more often about their families, interests, hobbies, and weekend plans, and whenever possible, recognizing them for various accomplishments as the company was fast moving and the assembly line professionals were a major cog in that wheel. If you talk to Bill about that style of walking the line, he'll say, "I remember someone wrote a book back then, and people started talking about this strategy of how to 'manage by walking around.' I thought, *Well heck, I've been doing that for years.*"

Bill also loved his executive role with the company and really didn't have further aspirations to get out of the manufacturing side of the shop. His demonstrations of gratitude with these professionals were genuine, and he never expected some sort of pat on the back in return. Bill respected them as people and respected and appreciated their expertise.

However, no one "walked around" Bill at his level. That didn't affect his passion and drive for excellence and energy to show gratitude. In fact, he'll tell you that's not something he needed; there were too many other people he felt should be recognized on the floor, those who were actually building the computers.

PERFORMANCE POINT

Do you assume, as you read about Bill, that when you get to an executive level, you will then switch gears and start showing gratitude?

ⓘ ERROR WARNING

Many solid professionals believe that when they get to management, they'll turn on the gratitude "switch" and start recognizing other people at their workplace. This error is a monumental one. First off, it's hard to get promoted if executives notice you have a hard time celebrating and crediting others. And if you slide by, you'll feel even more pressure to seek credit and recognition due to your inexperience and immaturity in a more pressure-filled role. Start showing gratitude now! You'll appreciate me for this. (I had to do it.)

This is one of the hardest concepts to grasp. The argument against me would start, "Well then, if everyone only focuses on showing others gratitude instead of thinking about how much they're appreciated...," please finish that sentence—and we've arrived at the true power of gratitude.

Need help? If everyone focused on gratitude, everyone would feel appreciated. The numbers don't lie.

Back to Bill. While he was an All-Star without a doubt, his consistency in gratitude, along with many other skills in this book, allowed him to lead his division through one of the most pivotal times in computer history, overcoming a huge obstacle on the path toward accomplishing the monumental achievement of beating the market leader at the time, IBM, and being the company to produce the fastest portable computer on the market in 1987, garnering a spot in *Fortune* magazine that featured the new state-of-the-art computer and the key team members pictured behind it. Bill is in that picture. Bill's name wasn't mentioned in the article, nor did he ask to be in the front row of the picture. To Bill, there were other key people on that team who really made it happen. Bill said he really didn't know the significance of the moment at the time: "We just built machines."

Like Bill, during my college coaching days, coaches would often share strategies about showing gratitude to their players in such a way that players felt fairly recognized. A successful coach who was asked to present at a national coaching convention shared that he kept a laminated note card with all his players' names in his pocket, and he would tally mark anytime he connected and showed gratitude to a player, with a goal of personally approaching each player during the week. I don't think it's a coincidence that he was so successful, he was chosen to present in front of three thousand aspiring baseball coaches.

Luckily, laminated paper isn't necessary anymore, as software can track who in a company hasn't received recognition so that we gratitude givers can begin spreading the secret.

In meeting with a culture committee of nonmanagement staff for a company with this type of software, they requested access to those names of employees not receiving recognition. They desired to observe and make sure to "catch them" doing well so they could offer appreciation. Not one of these committee members wondered how often they themselves were recognized. This committee is always one of the company's most engaged groups, who care greatly about the culture and core values of their company, realizing they are a part of something meaningful. Why? It's pretty clear: They focused on giving gratitude, not concerning themselves with how much they received it. They are All-Stars in the skill of gratitude.

Gratitude Self-Reflection

This self-evaluation is for *you*. If you want to share with a trusted peer or leader to build accountability toward your newly acquired skills, that is a bonus. At the very least, if you are choosing to make a run at being an All-Star, personal accountability can start here. Decide which number below applies most to you at this point and circle the number.

1. I only concentrate on whether or not I am getting appreciated by others at work.
2. I'll be honest: I see where I could improve in this skill, and I don't normally do even what professionals do in this area.
3. The professional behaviors and "errors" best describe how I approach this skill.
4. I relate more to the All-Star skills, behaviors, and actions. I am very intentional, consistent, and specific with gratitude.
5. I've been doing these All-Star actions to display my gratitude for three to five years.

The Closer - Bullpen Bullets

- ★ **Start Giving Recognition Daily:** Make it a habit to personally thank or acknowledge at least one colleague each day—out loud, in person, or through a thoughtful message—to strengthen connection and engagement.
- ★ **Show Gratitude Before You Feel Appreciated:** When you start feeling undervalued, shift focus by recognizing others' contributions first—because giving gratitude increases your own sense of meaning and fulfillment.
- ★ **Deliver Gratitude in Person:** Step away from your desk or inbox, and express appreciation face-to-face, showing sincerity and building genuine relationships that stand out in any workplace.

6

COMMUNICATION

I have a bad habit that's been very difficult to break.

I'm very comfortable with meeting people I don't know, working the room, introducing myself, and networking. But I can't tell you how many times I've introduced myself to someone, learned their name, gotten into a five-to-seven-minute conversation—and realized I've already forgotten their name.

Now, I know about half the people reading this book suffer from the same kind of memory lapse, but it's still a difficult habit to break. It's something I have to work on continuously.

This is one of the main reasons why I typically say introverts make better networkers. Why? Because they tend to listen better than people like me.

As I mentioned earlier, I'm the prototypical extrovert, a somewhat scatterbrained creative. Not creative in the artistic sense, but if you know the Six Working Geniuses, one of my *Geniuses* is inventing. I can come up with some pretty solid ideas for solving problems. And remembering people's names? That could help me solve those problems a lot faster.

At this point, you're probably confused about what any of this has to do with communication—maybe with the exception of listening. But I start here because, as professionals striving to become All-Stars, we hold on to this amazing delusion: While we can't remember someone's name five minutes after meeting them, we somehow believe that dropping by someone's office or cubicle and saying something about a project will suffice as communicating the information.

Let's just stop right there. If we can't remember a person's name, how can we expect them to remember that we told them something important in passing? Worse, when they forget it, we act like it's their fault.

This—right here—is where All-Stars set themselves apart: in their ability to communicate strategically.

Yes, I know, communicating strategically sounds like more corporate jargon. Maybe so, but this is corporate jargon that is a necessary skill.

To share an oft-quoted motto, whose origin is disputed as coming from various business and military sources, "Tell them what you're going to tell them. Then tell them. Then tell them what you told them."

Let's go back to my name-forgetting problem. Imagine if you had two really good happy-hour "wingmen." When I say good wingmen, that means they know how to network during happy hours and never put you in a position that puts you in a negative light with someone you are connecting with. An All-Star wingman move, if you will, during a networking event goes as follows:

They see you talking to someone whose name is Sharon and walk up to introduce themselves to the person you just met. Like All-Star networkers, they don't put you in a position to introduce them to Sharon; they lead with their own names.

Your first friend says, "Hi, I'm Liz Townsend. Good to meet you!"

The person you're talking to replies, "Hi, good to meet you, Liz. I'm Sharon Wilgus."

Boom. That's the second time you've heard her name.

A few minutes later, your second wingman walks up: "Hi, I'm Rod Branch."

Sharon responds, "Great to meet you, Rod. I'm Sharon Wilgus," again sharing her name.

That's the third time you've heard her name—and now, odds are, it's locked in. You'll remember it forever.

No, this chapter isn't intended to focus on All-Star happy hour networking tactics, but the concept highlights where we can make significant errors in communicating with our colleagues and superiors.

Imagine how many breakdowns happen around far more complex projects than remembering a name. Yet many professionals have a tendency to communicate something once and believe that should suffice. That's why the majority of this chapter is focused on how to communicate like an All-Star.

Below is a quick list of errors many professionals make in communication. As you read them, and perhaps admit to yourself that you do some of them, understand that All-Stars rarely make these errors in strategic communication. I won't go into deep detail—because you'll very likely recognize these behaviors the second I name them.

Seven Communication Errors Professionals Make

1. The CYA Email

You know exactly what this is. The "cover your ***" email. Without forecasting or alerting your audience to this email coming, you send a critical update or need for information on a project believing that's enough to say, "I communicated."

It's common for professionals—especially those who are actually good at their jobs—to say, "Well, I sent an email about it," when someone on the team wasn't aware of the update or data request.

First, you know it annoys you when other people say it to you, and second, it's not enough to just "send the email" if you want to be an All-Star.

2. The Vague Subject Line

Urgent doesn't mean anything if everything is marked urgent. When I work alongside brilliant executives who likely get twice the emails that I do, I know they don't have time to dig into unclear subject lines.

If I really need their attention, the subject line will say something like this: "ACTION NEEDED: Budget Approval for Q3 Events."

And I've likely already told them in a hallway, meeting, or Teams message that this is coming. So the subject line is the second time they've heard it. And the message in the email itself is the third.

If you're just sharing info? Great. But don't send an email out of the blue stating you need action, with a vague subject line, and expect a quick response. There is a very good chance you'll need to follow up somehow.

3. Unclear Use of Pings, Emails, and Drop-Ins

"Ping" is apparently the semi-official term for Teams messages. One of my coordinators always says, "I pinged you," or "I emailed you," and I recently realized—those are two *very* different things.

All-stars use different tools for different purposes:

- **Teams/Slack**—quick updates or real-time messages understanding no guarantee of a quick response. (Typically informal.)
- **Email**—more formal, with documented details; good response time for action items is usually around twenty-four hours. A follow-up is needed past that because they are likely missed.
    - **CC Email**—keeping someone publicly in the loop, but not expecting action, a response, or even a thorough read of it. (Use correctly.)
    - **BCC Email**—allowing someone, likely the one who brought you into the conversation, to know you have taken the ball on the thread but are saving them from future conversations, unnecessarily clogging their inbox. (On a very rare occasion, if ever, used to keep someone secretly in the loop. Consult senior management or HR if you believe this is necessary and tread lightly.)
- **Texts**—urgent and/or personal items
- **Calls**—real-time decisions. All-stars typically leave voice mails and at the very least follow with a text if they don't reach the intended person.

- **Office/Cubicle drop-ins**—presence and connection. The two-minute drill referenced in chapter 4 on relationships. Visiting various coworkers and leaders to genuinely check in on them, not to be confused with an "office hit-and-run" (see below).

4. The Office Hit-and-Run

Totally different from a presence-building drop-in, the hit-and-run is when a professional tries to get quick approval or dump information in a passing moment that really should've been a proper meeting or documented discussion.

It's a signal of poor planning.

5. Starting Where You Left Off

Whether it's your boss, peer, or report, this is a classic mistake: picking up the conversation like no time has passed.

The other person has had a dozen meetings since then. You've had time to think about where you want to go—they haven't.

All-stars do what Netflix does: "Previously on (pick your binge watch series) . . ." They offer a quick recap so everyone's on the same page before continuing. My wife implores me to "skip the recap" because she just wants to get to the new stuff. Sometimes I need the recap if it's been a while because I can't remember where we left off. And so does your work audience.

All of your favorite subscription service TV series don't assume you remember everything. Don't expect your coworkers to either.

6. A Hybrid of #4 and #5: The Low-Importance Email "Check-in"

I need a better name for this one. But here's what I mean: Someone pokes their head into your office and says, "Did you see my email?" And there is no context given with the ask, nor has there been any previous conversation about what was coming, and even worse, it's not urgent or important. The offender has used email like a text message, hasn't received a response in a time frame they would prefer, and clearly has little else to do.

I probably give an unwelcome look when that happens. What I'm *thinking* is, *If you were going to take advantage of my open door and walk into my office to ask if I saw your email, why did you send the email in the first place instead of just telling me or asking in person?*

What I actually say is something polite like, "No, I haven't gotten to it yet."

Again, don't feel bad—we've all done this. This book exists to point out these things so you can adjust. If you're going to send an email, have a reason for doing it besides just convenience. Refer back to section 3 above regarding unclear use of emails.

7. Waiting to Talk Instead of Listening (Really Listening)

In getting various feedback from leaders about communication, a CFO I worked with emphasized this skill. And you'll recognize this one. Staring at someone's mouth moving while you are concentrating on how you will deliver your next compelling point. Then realizing somewhere along the way that you have not heard anything they have said in the past two minutes in order to truly understand and appreciate their perspective. The most intriguing part of this error many professionals make is it is very easy for the person delivering the message to tell that you're doing this. It's easy to determine if the "listener" is checked out because they are forming their next point to deliver their case, not working to understand the other point of view. Listening and understanding is communication.

King Solomon's proverb probably says it best: "Fools find no pleasure in understanding but delight in airing their own opinions" (Proverbs 18:2).

So listen! Then pause and think about what you just heard, and then form your next points. No one will think less of you for taking the time to appreciate the perspective you just heard and collect your thoughts.

RACI: A Simple Tool for Strategic Communication

A great project management tool for project meeting updates is the RACI tool. However, I have also found it to be very helpful when trying to communicate updates and issues at an All-Star level. Professionals often leave various stakeholders out because they often think in just linear or proximal terms, meaning they typically think about the direct teams they work with (linear) or the people near them most often as the work progresses (proximal).

I'll give you a quick example. Have you ever had an encounter with someone in your office or workplace where the second you saw them, you were reminded you haven't communicated something that they may be expecting or that you may owe them? That's a momentary "proximal" connection. *What team is working on this, or who is working close to me on this project?* Thinking about people in the buckets of the RACI model is a sound thought process, and All-Star communicators often don't leave the following people out when they are attempting to communicate broadly.

RACI stands for those who are

- **Responsible**
- **Accountable**
- **Consulted**
- **Informed**

You don't have to be a certified project manager (PMP) to understand how this can help you structure your communication.

Most professionals communicate a bit more haphazardly. All-stars don't. All-stars use strategic thinking and ask the following questions:

- Who needs to know this?
- Who needs to act?
- Who should be consulted?
- Who should simply be informed or in the loop?

Before you hit send or when you are preparing your updates on a project or initiative, ask yourself these questions. This is an All-Star skill.

All-Star CEO Communication

I once worked for a CEO who modeled this better than anyone. It was during the moment I resigned. Let's be clear: This is a moment when I actually resigned, as opposed to what I experienced from my exit from baseball coaching (see chapter 4, "Relationships").

I loved my job. I loved the people. I simply had a strong personal reason to make a move: to be closer to family. But this was going to be a surprise to him and the company. I sat down in his office and, through tears, told him I was leaving the company as I had an opportunity to be closer to home.

His first question: "Is everyone okay?"

Sidebar: That tells you everything you need to know about this leader. He didn't ask, "Can I change your mind?" or "Who are you going to work for?" He cared about my family.

When I told him I was resigning, only four people knew at that point—him, my wife, my future boss, and me included. After being assured everyone close to me was healthy and not in danger, a switch flipped, and I could see him immediately think through a communication strategy for the organization.

In a year when he had made a number of executive changes, he didn't want this to seem like "another departure" in an executive shuffle. He didn't want a wave of questions to distract the team. So we discussed best timing and overall message.

Looking back, he may have not formally thought through the RACI list, but he was thinking through who should be informed of my resignation and when. He was walking through strategic communication content and timing. We even wrote the company announcement email together. It was thoughtful, clear, warm, and preemptive. That's how All-Stars think through and communicate big news. This gentleman had been operating at this All-Star level for many years, so he'd easily make it to the Hall of Fame as far as CEOs are concerned, if there is a Hall of Fame for that.

If You're Going to Deliver Bad News—Go First

When you mess something up—and we all do—you need to tell your boss before someone else does. If someone else tells them first because you were hoping the boss wouldn't find out, you'll likely lose some trust. Read the Planning chapter which references the effectiveness of hope as a tactic.

PERFORMANCE POINT

Recall the last time you discovered you'd screwed up pretty bad. What was your initial reaction?

ⓘ ERROR WARNING

If your instinct is hoping you can avoid telling your superior, or hoping no one notices, or finding outside circumstances that contributed to you making the error, you are not too far off many professionals. Many professionals in the workplace minimize or deflect mistakes to avoid accountability.

All-stars wear it, and they make sure their boss hears it from them first.

Put yourself in your boss's shoes. And if you're a parent or have a significant other, you probably can understand. If your kid fails a test, do you want to hear it from the school or from your child? Or if your spouse or significant other encountered an ex at a restaurant or bar, is there not a difference between your loved one telling you versus one of your friends who saw them across the room sending you a text the next day about it, or worse, a picture of them talking?

Same with your manager. And if you can't trust your boss enough to be honest with them about the failure, you're either wrongly vilifying them, or you didn't evaluate your boss enough during your interview process and you're likely in the wrong job. Ooh, did that sting? And before you take that leap and start looking for a new job, have you ever tried to bring bad news to them before they heard about it? If you fail to do so because you assume your boss will react poorly, you are making an error, and this error can knock you below the professional level, more like an entry-level, developing employee. Holding anything back from people, especially your leadership, because of how you think they will respond versus true, firsthand experience is nothing more than amateur. Give your boss a shot first in order to validate or invalidate your assumption. And if you've made it this far in the book and still say, "But you don't know my boss," that's more typical of developing employees than seasoned professionals. And very far from All-Star. You'll need to improve this mindset and likely your *relationship* skills with your boss as well if you want to advance.

Here's the thing: All-stars know that transparency and vulnerability earn trust and confidence faster than perfection ever could. Secondly, as my CEO says, "If you can get to me first, that gives me time to think through my reaction when someone else brings it to me and I can be your air cover." And if you are new to the term 'air cover,' your immediate challenge is to go ask your superior, "What does it mean for you to offer me air cover?" when something goes wrong and I tell you about it before anyone approaches you?" They will explain it, then respect you highly for learning about strategic communication.

Sideways Communication: An Underrated Skill

Most professionals know how to manage and communicate up, meaning they have figured out how to navigate the relationship and communication strategy with their superiors.

All-stars additionally build solid horizontal relationships by being good sideways communicators as well—this is the communication with peers and colleagues who don't report to them and whom they don't report to.

And it's hard. It's awkward. Especially if you're competitive.

But the All-Star peers are those who show up, who check in with each other, find out what is going on in each other's world, share credit with each other, and who say, "I've got your back," because they know what you are going through, and because All-Stars understand the high value on sideways communication.

I've made the error of undervaluing and failing to be a good sideways communicator in the past, and it created significant challenges to my growth. I had a difficult time building a strong connection with a gentleman who started at the same time as I did at a previous company. This didn't make sense at all given we were roughly the same age, had a very similar work ethic and positivity, and worked for the same boss for a couple of years, but we just didn't engage each other much at all. I knew there was plenty to communicate about when you are on the same team, meaning we shared the same level on the organization chart reporting up to the same director—not that we had similar jobs; he was in training; I was in HR. So don't think of team as department, like HR; we were on the same team because we were on the same level, serving the same leader. In *The Five Dysfunctions of a Team*, Patrick Lencioni highlights the importance of having the most trust built up and loyalty to your "first team," which means those on the same level.[13] I definitely did not have loyalty toward him because there was no vulnerable communication and connection between us. I regret this. He was ultimately promoted to the executive team before me. And he deserved it. I was a bit envious from a competitive standpoint but knew in my heart he'd earned the promotion.

PERFORMANCE POINT

Do you have a posture of envy or jealousy when a peer gets promoted?

ⓘ ERROR WARNING

Envy or jealousy is a strong sign that you've failed to communicate often with the peer you're jealous of. The more you engage and communicate, the better your relationship gets, the more humanity you share, and likely, the more you will see a promotion coming and be happy for them.

Sometime later, I also was promoted to the executive team, and we were back in the same circles, on the same "team." One day, at our first off-site executive meeting, he told me he had heard from other leaders in years past that they sometimes saw me as a "shape-shifter"—someone trying to be different things to different people solely for their approval—and it impacted how they would engage me. He apologized that he'd held on to that information and not told me earlier. While I appreciated his apology, that wasn't his fault at all.

[13] Patrick Lencioni, *The Five Dysfunctions of a Team: A Leadership Fable* (San Francisco: Jossey-Bass, 2002), 137.

What I wish I'd done was get lunch with him at least once in a while. Or check in monthly. Or just send an occasional text message that said, "How's life?"

That could've changed the game. I know him well enough now to know that had I engaged him in genuine communication as a peer, he would have told me those things much earlier, where I would have been able to salvage other relationships earlier.

All-stars will have regular, consistent, collaborative communication with peers. Professionals are cordial and respectful, but not likely to engage at a level that builds strong "sideways" workplace interactions.

Conflict Isn't the Enemy—Silence Is

I've had disagreements in meetings. Passionate ones. The kind where someone slams the table. This is raw, but often good, communication.

PERFORMANCE POINT

What do you go through emotionally or how do you respond when a coworker, leader, or direct report gets loud, passionate, or somewhat aggressive with their tone?

ⓘ ERROR WARNING

Many professionals will shut down here. And it may depend on whether the person is displaying assertiveness or aggression. Being in a room with this kind of conflict is a tough position to be in, and without knowing how to handle this, so many great employees can't effectively process what they immediately feel when tensions get escalated. They take it personally even though nothing personal is said. All-stars handle these types of communication with levelheadedness, if not appreciation. They know it's part of business.

Very recent to writing this chapter, a peer got heated, direct, with a couple profanities mixed in, sharing their opinion of a project I was working on. I followed up the next day and said, "Thanks for being genuine with me. I appreciate that."

He apologized for his passion. He didn't need to apologize, and I told him that. I want that passion. I want the honesty. I always prefer knowing where people are coming from. It's healthy.

All-stars don't try to avoid conflict. They appreciate it, and they try to *understand* it, and the really good All-Stars actually mine for it. Assertiveness in the book *The EQ Edge* is described as being comprised of three basic components: (1) the ability to express feelings (for example, to accept and express anger); (2) the ability to express beliefs and thoughts openly (being able to voice opinions, disagree, and take a definite stand, even if it is emotionally difficult to do so and even if you have something to lose by doing so); and (3) the ability to stand up for personal rights (not allowing others to bother you or take advantage of you).[14]

Communicating like an All-Star isn't about being perfect. It's about being intentional.

Use the right tools. Repeat important messages. Own your mistakes. Communicate to build peer relationships. Don't dump and dash. Appreciate conflict and passionate communication, both your own and others. Most importantly, listen.

And please—for the love of all that is good in the workplace—don't walk into someone's office just to ask if they saw your email.

[14] Steven J. Stein and Howard E. Book, *The EQ Edge: Emotional Intelligence and Your Success* (Jossey-Bass, 2011), 105.

Communication Self-Reflection

This self-evaluation is for *you*. If you want to share with a trusted peer or leader to build accountability toward your newly acquired skills, that is a bonus. At the very least, if you are choosing to make a run at being an All-Star, personal accountability can start here. Decide which number below applies most to you at this point and circle the number.

1. The extent of my communication is answering questions someone asks me or emailing people when I need something.
2. I see where I could improve in this skill. I often make the errors listed and have never considered strategy in how I communicate, but I see where it would help me.
3. The professional behaviors and "errors" best describe how I approach this skill. I've been often described as a good communicator, but I could fine-tune and adopt the strategies in this chapter to level up my strategy.
4. I seldom make the communication errors listed and even occasionally prompt others to enhance their ability to communicate. I feel I have good control of getting action and response regardless of the level I am communicating with.
5. I've been adopting these methods for at least three to five years where effective communication in the workplace seems second nature.

The Closer - Bullpen Bullets

- ★ **Communicate Strategically, Not Spontaneously:** Before sending a message or giving an update, pause, and ask, *Who needs to know, who needs to act, who should be consulted, and who should simply be informed?*
- ★ **Repeat and Reinforce Key Messages:** Don't assume one mention is enough—communicate important information multiple times and through multiple channels to ensure it's understood and remembered.
- ★ **Own Mistakes and Go First with Bad News:** When something goes wrong, tell your boss or team immediately—transparency builds more trust and credibility than perfection ever will.

7

INNOVATION

I want to take a moment in this part of the book, before we dive into innovation, to be perfectly clear about something—again. One of the CEOs I spoke with before writing this book reminded me, "Jared, you have to make sure you're not communicating to everyone who picks up this book that they're required to be an All-Star or that we only desire people to be All-Stars, because we need professionals too. Our companies are successful because of the professionals." There are people in companies who are not in a season where they can be an All-Star right now or have no desire to be an All-Star, but they're still extremely good professionals. As you go through these chapters and self-assess whether you're performing the skills at a professional level or an All-Star level, you must also consider whether you have a desire and are willing to pursue being an All-Star, knowing that it's impossible for a company to have only All-Stars in their workforce. Just like artists and athletes, most are professional, few become All-Stars.

However, there are likely very few professionals who don't desire to be All-Stars who would pick up this book. But for those of you who are proud, hard-working professionals—those of you who love being a professional but have no desire to do all the All-Star thing in this season of your life and are still valuable members of your workforce—feel free to send me a LinkedIn message privately. I'd love to personally thank you for what you do every day for your company. Remember you are valued and important.

As I just mentioned, professionals are reliable and very good at what they do. While there may be a few jobs that have an innovative expectation tied to them, most professionals are not required to be innovative. Innovation is the act of bringing new things—new ideas, new methods—to a role, department, or company that add value.

Innovation is often directly impacted and enhanced by your involvement. Most professionals are involved with organizations, committees, lunch-and-learns, or conferences that give opportunities to stay up to date in their industry or practice and network with peers. However, involvement doesn't necessarily mean that you're exercising the skill of innovation; it simply gives you more resources and ability to do so. If you are not involved, start now, because a lack of involvement isn't even an error professionals make. That's why the skill of involvement doesn't appear in the All-Star skill list.

One of my peers at a large publicly traded company said, "I want and encourage my people all the time to bring new things and new ways to my office, to challenge how I do things. That's what stretches us and makes us better."

As I write this book, AI is low-hanging fruit for professionals to spend some extra time to learn and find ways to integrate it into what their organization does. AI will be a path for many professionals to become All-Star innovators if they take advantage *now*.

If you learn the skill and ability to be innovative in your role as a professional, you will drift toward that All-Star level. But fair warning: All-stars get promoted to roles where the skill of innovation becomes an expectation, rather than just a feather in your cap.

It's Your Job

I've been in one of these role for years now. Once, I was sitting in one of my monthly updates with a CEO when he suggested a wellness program he had heard about from his own executive peer group. I told him it sounded pretty cool, and I'd look into it to see what the logistics, administrative burden, and cost were and report back. Weeks later, when he and I sat down in his office and went through the cost-benefit analysis of embedding this program into our workforce, we came to a "green light" decision to move ahead and adopt the program; I was rather excited about the positive change this would be for our workforce. Right before I left to start executing the task, he looked at me and said, "You know, Jared, it's actually your job to bring these types of ideas to me—not mine to find them out." How about that for direct feedback on my innovation skill? More importantly, he was right.

So there you have it. As I said before, I am now in one of those roles where innovation is an expectation. And that's what executives in your organization are looking for right now—those people who bring possibilities and potential to them to consider, because those are the All-Stars who are likely to exercise innovation when it's "expected" in the role they get promoted to.

PERFORMANCE POINT

How many new ideas have you discovered outside your organization that could benefit the company as a whole? Have you brought them to leadership? Whether or not they were implemented, have you been the one to bring them to the table?

ⓘ ERROR WARNING

Passivity is the enemy of innovation. Professionals will always research when asked by their superiors to look into something. Researching is not innovating. Innovation is cradle-to-grave action—you stay on top of trends, possibilities, pipe dreams, crazy ideas, and everything in between to determine if, as I like to put it, "it's got legs" in your organization, meaning it's got a good chance of success. Innovation happens off the clock. But just like any sport, hobby, or skill, All-Stars are always practicing and honing their abilities more often than professionals.

This doesn't mean you have to bore yourself with trade magazines from nine to eleven every night. But I happen to take the city bus into work on occasion, and I am shocked to see how many professionals play Candy Crush, watch their Netflix series, or scroll Instagram for forty-five minutes on the bus ride in. I respect their desire for some downtime before or after work, but make no mistake: All-stars are using that time to listen to an industry or business podcast, read a scholarly journal, or catch up on the latest article from the *Harvard Business Review*, whatever it is that gives them insight into what's going on in their business world.

Some of you probably worry about this skill of innovation, thinking you may not be creative enough. Don't sweat that. There are enough creatives, true market innovators out there who you can stay close to, follow, or read up on, who will keep you as close to the cutting edge as you need to be. Unless your CEO is a major risk taker, most CEOs and organizations would prefer to be early adopters, similar to how Simon Sinek refers to the Law of Diffusion Innovation.[15] It's a rare CEO who likes to blaze trails, but what they definitely don't want is to be forced to change because they weren't aware of where the winds were blowing. And that's where you come in as the innovator and an All-Star in your organization.

Here's where innovation gets tricky—the application. This chapter has covered bringing new ideas to leaders that aren't already happening in your organization, so those leaders will consider, accept, and begin executing those ideas. One of my pet peeves in corporate professionalism and leadership books is sharing a good idea but not really telling you *how* to implement it. So let's get into it. How do you innovate in your organization?

---

[15] Simon Sinek, *Start with Why: How Great Leaders Inspire Everyone to Take Action*, 15th Anniversary Ed. (Portfolio, 2011).

If you haven't already been able to intuit this before now, I'll be clear: You cannot be an All-Star if you have a forty-hour-a-week mindset about your career. Yes, I just said it. Once again, if your life and career goals hinge on a forty-hour workweek so you can have the "work-life balance" you desire, that's totally fine, and I commend you. But there are professionals around you who have a career and life desire to be at a higher level in their organization—to be an All-Star—and we can commend them too. But to be an innovator, it's not going to happen on a forty-hour workweek. Because in those forty hours, you have to do your day-to-day job. And in a complex role, there's no way you can get everything done in just forty hours a week. But I digress.

Think

To be innovative in your organization, the first skill you must exercise is critical thinking. You have to set aside time for ample critical thinking. Yes, time to think. One of the most common frustrations I hear from executives is the lack of critical thinking in their organization. That's why so many professionals think they're All-Stars when they're not—they're professionals who are good at their job, sometimes great at what they do, but they're still not All-Stars.

Executives see their All-Stars and are at peace with them because they know they are doing a lot of critical thinking. All-stars think through what's out there, what's next, where their organization is going. What types of things have we implemented that have been successful? What types of things have we not implemented that could possibly work and bring value? What types of things am I hearing out there that would be an absolute train wreck in our organization? If an executive comes and asks you, "Have you heard of this?" you would've already vetted it, and you know where the challenges and roadblocks would be.

That's just scratching the surface of the types of critical thinking and research that All-Stars do. If you're reading this and thinking, *I don't think about these things on a regular basis*, that's okay. That's self-awareness. You're just not yet an All-Star innovator. Executives want people who ask these questions and do this type of research without being prompted. That's what innovation is. And you can start now.

I don't know what's going on in your organization, but you definitely need to know what's happening in your organization, what your peers are doing, and what your industry leaders are doing. Think through these things—what could be implemented, how you could strike up certain conversations, how to get sponsorship from executives, and how you could get new initiatives successfully imbedded in your department or organization. I hope you're beginning to see why critical thinking time—intentional time dedicated to it—is absolutely necessary to be considered one of the innovative people in your organization.

PERFORMANCE POINT

Think back to a time when you found a really innovative approach to a project or process that you thought would bring value to your organization, but the executive shot it down quickly—almost as if they didn't even listen. Before you brought it up, how much critical thinking about your organization did you do? Things like financial position, revenue, your own company's climate and culture, appetite for change, previous attempts at innovation, resources necessary to push that innovation forward versus the resources likely available, tenure of the executive team, leadership team, your team—all of these factors play into how an idea is received.

ⓘ ERROR WARNING

It's inevitable that every time I don't consider the status of the organization, my idea and I will get escorted out of the office quickly—not in a termination sort of way, but that idea will be thrown out fast. Professionals can have good ideas, but often they don't consider timing based on the factors outside their immediate company sphere or environment.

Every time I don't consider the viability of the idea for my specific organization, I miss the mark. Innovation requires change, and change requires change management, which requires an organization's appetite for it. All those factors I listed go into an organization's capacity for change. Some of you work for huge ships with small rudders that turn the ship slowly—that's okay, but you have to understand how initiatives, innovation, and change work in those organizations. The only way you can really understand that is to think through previous changes and execute similarly. That said, some of you work for fast-moving organizations. And I'll tell you this: I've worked for both types of organizations, and the scariest ones can be the ones that move swiftly. Sometimes I long for the days of the small rudder and big ship because I knew I had plenty of time to manage, communicate, and effect great change since it wasn't going to happen fast. I could think things through and build more certainty that an idea will be successful; fast organizations will let you take the risk—and the fall.

When you work for a more entrepreneurial firm, you have to have everything ready when you discuss potential initiatives or changes. There's a chance the idea is so good that your leadership may just tell you to execute it by the end of the month. And if you haven't critically thought it through, it could stain your ability to innovate effectively and strategically. In entrepreneurial-style organizations that embrace fast change, they trust you've done the critical thinking. You may fail miserably if you haven't.

Go with 80%

Let's fast-forward and assume you will start putting critical thinking into your skill set. At some point in your quest to be an innovator, your critical thinking will have to stop, and you'll have to make a decision to propose, which is the second skill you need in innovation. Here's where I'll lose a lot of people: The action and skill of decision making has to begin when you're about 80 percent sure your idea will work. So many professionals want to have all their questions answered, to have 100 percent certainty that something will work or is planned out perfectly. That's not innovation at all. Leaders know new ideas and processes are never guaranteed successes—especially executives.

Some of you may have a leader or executive who suffers from "paralysis by analysis." They never make a decision unless they're 100 percent sure. This likely frustrates you, and I get it, I've been there. There are two reasons for this: (1) They're not innovative and they're not risk-takers, or (2) they don't want to do anything that could potentially risk their position. I have worked with someone like this, though the organization we worked for was more risk-averse overall as well, so that likely factored into this person's pause when I brought ideas up for consideration.

If you're 80 percent sure an initiative is going to work, and there are only a few things that could cause it to fail, it's time to bring it to light to your leadership. Don't get stuck trying to solve every possible problem before moving forward. If you're 80 percent sure, you know those potential problems are likely not going to happen. Your leaders and executives know this too—better yet, if they know you're aware of the potential problems, they'll know you've done your critical thinking.

A mentor of mine, an executive in the banking software industry, once told me a great saying she got from her father, Don Peterson of Macksville, Kansas, who was a banking wizard. Don would often say, "The worst thing you can do is not make the decision to move forward, even with some uncertainty. Make the decision, move forward, and if you realize it's a bad decision, make a different one."

Handle "No"

Lastly, to be a great innovator, you have to have the skill to be okay with hearing no from your executives. So many professionals bring their ideas to the table, get shut down, and—in sports terminology for a sore loser—they take their ball and go home because their feelings are hurt. This is business. This is organizational success. You need to understand that your leaders see the battlefield differently than you, and there are parts of that battlefield you can't see. You have to trust them on that because, at the end of the day, if they make the decision, it's on them. They'll credit you with the innovation, but make no mistake: It's on their head if the project goes badly (or "pear shaped," as one of my executives loves to say).

Don't take the no's personally. Initiatives aren't your children. Innovation isn't your baby. As an All-Star, it's your job—or it will ultimately be your job when you get promoted—to innovate. That's it. Professionals get their feelings hurt all the time because their idea wasn't put into practice. All-stars know it's their job to bring those ideas to light, to bring opportunities to bear. And if their innovation isn't accepted, they want to learn why: Was it bad timing? Did I miss something? And their executive will give them the answer.

As you'll learn, every time you present an idea, you're honing your ability to innovate. You're becoming a better innovator in your organization. If you're open to feedback from your executives and genuinely want to understand where your idea doesn't fit, ask them. Tell them that you felt you critically thought through everything—so you want to know what was missing. You'll learn from them. And I guarantee they'll appreciate the fact that you're trying to think through what could bring value to the organization while also being successful in your day-to-day job. Everyone wants that person. Because then executives know they have an All-Star innovator in the making. Start becoming that person.

Innovation Self-Reflection

This self-evaluation is for *you*. If you want to share with a trusted peer or leader to build accountability toward your newly acquired skills, that is a bonus. At the very least, if you are choosing to make a run at being an All-Star, personal accountability can start here. Decide which number below applies most to you at this point and circle the number.

1. I'm not an idea person, and I don't care to research in my spare time.
2. I'll be honest: I see where I could improve in this skill, and I'd like to start discovering new ideas to bring to the organization and thinking things through; I've just always been waiting to be asked.
3. The professional behaviors and "errors" best describe how I approach this skill. I can research and bring sound change management strategy, but I rarely take intentional time to think. I also take more time than I should bringing ideas to the table, fearing they'll fail.
4. I relate more to the All-Star skills, behaviors, and actions when it comes to innovation. I often spend commuting time or weekends thinking through initiatives or potential improvements for our organization.
5. I've been doing these All-Star actions with innovation for three to five years.

The Closer - Bullpen Bullets

- ★ **Set aside time for critical thinking each week** to study trends, ideas, and opportunities in your industry so you can proactively bring well-vetted innovations to your leaders.
- ★ **Decide and act when you're 80 percent confident** in an idea's success instead of waiting for perfect certainty—progress beats paralysis in innovation.
- ★ **Seek feedback, not validation, when your ideas get rejected** so you can learn from the no, refine your thinking, and strengthen your ability to innovate strategically.

8

EMOTIONS

After the Battle of Gettysburg, President Abraham Lincoln was furious that General George Meade failed to aggressively pursue the retreating Confederate army. He wrote a letter to the General expressing his deep frustration—but never sent it.

He tucked it away in a drawer, later inscribing the envelope with a simple note: "Never sent or signed."[16]

Lincoln was known for his exceptional ability to manage his emotions. Without a doubt, he was an All-Star-level president.

I found it ironic how difficult it was to start writing this chapter. Look into my background and you'll find I'm a certified executive coach. I'm also certified in emotional intelligence coaching through the EQ-i 2.0 assessment—the most validated emotional intelligence tool in the world. I teach this material often at my firm and coach executives across industries on emotional intelligence. As I am writing this chapter, I am

[16] Abraham Lincoln, unsent letter to Gen. George Meade, July 1863, Library of Congress, https://www.battlefields.org/learn/primary-sources/lincolns-unsent-letter-george-meade.

also planning to be a guest on a podcast designed for pastors in their leadership development journey. So, it amused me that I didn't feel particularly motivated to write this chapter. I have an uncle who always used to say, "A pleasure that remains does not remain a pleasure." Maybe I need a break from talking or writing about emotional intelligence, but it won't be soon.

Because one truth remains: A professional who learns to harness and leverage their emotions can quickly become an All-Star.

That said, there are already many excellent books on emotional intelligence. I'll do my best not to be redundant but instead offer practical scenarios and distinctions between being a professional and being an All-Star as it relates to emotions in the workplace. Sometimes, that distinction comes down to one's ability to manage—or reluctance to manage—emotional expression.

And yes, I use the word *reluctance* deliberately. Many professionals shy away from any emotion. But that isn't always the best approach. I believe one of the most valuable growth areas for professionals is in realizing how their unmanaged or unrecognized emotions can create unintended consequences for others—consequences they might not even be aware of.

Right on Red

Let me offer a simple example.

I live in Houston, Texas—known for its sprawling freeways, relentless traffic, and, depending on whom you ask, drivers who are either "fast and loose" or "completely nuts." I'll let you decide which it is.

One particular behavior on Houston roads infuriates me—and yet I see its parallel in the workplace constantly.

Here's the scenario: Most of us know that turning right on red is legal in Houston and can save significant time during a commute. But picture this: You're approaching a red light on a multilane road. You're in the right lane, intending to turn right. But the car in front of you, also approaching the red light, is going straight. Instead of staying in the center or left lane behind a few other cars, that driver shifts into the right lane—blocking your ability to turn.

They do this just to be first in line at the red light. First! Not third. Not fourth. First.

It's infuriating. And the real kicker? I'd bet good money they have no idea they're blocking right-turning traffic behind them. They're not trying to be cruel. They simply aren't thinking about anyone but themselves in that moment.

What do I do if I pull up behind them?

Well, I drift my car to the right. I turn on my blinker—so they can clearly see it in their side mirror. Then, in my imagination, I lay on the horn and send them a message: *You inconsiderate, heartless, self-absorbed human being! How dare you?!* How is that for emotional expression!

But in reality? I rarely do anything. Occasionally, I'll edge right with my blinker on, but I never honk. That would be impulsive and show a complete lack of emotional control. Still, I feel the anger and I judge them harshly.

Until, of course, later that day.

I'm distracted. I'm at a red light. I pull into the right lane without thinking. I'm going straight. And wouldn't you know it—someone behind me wants to turn right. I've blocked them.

I didn't mean to. I wasn't being selfish. My mind was elsewhere. Life was happening.

Funny how that works.

This is a classic example of what Patrick Lencioni, in *The Five Dysfunctions of a Team*, calls the "fundamental attribution error"—the tendency to attribute other people's actions to their character and our own missteps to external circumstances.[17]

In that moment, my emotional frustration is fueled by the belief that the other driver is inconsiderate. But when I make the same mistake? I'm just human. Overwhelmed. Distracted by external circumstances.

This assumption of malicious intentions is one of the most common emotional management pitfalls I see in very good professionals frequently.

My sister-in-law, a dynamic pastor in Kansas, says it best: "Don't assign intent."

---

[17] Patrick Lencioni, *Overcoming The Five Dysfunctions of a Team: A Leadership Fable* (San Francisco: Jossey-Bass, 2005), 21.

Once you assign negative intent to someone else's action, you surrender your emotional control and often, productive emotional expression.

Professionals make emotional decisions all the time, and by "emotional," I mean decisions based on *inaccurate* or *misplaced* feelings. That doesn't mean it's wrong to feel something. But sometimes, our initial emotional reactions are simply wrong.

Let's take a workplace scenario.

You send a colleague a message via Microsoft Teams (or Slack, or any other chat app). You see the "Read" receipt or the eyeball indicating they read your message. They start typing. Then stop. And never respond.

What do you think in that moment?

PERFORMANCE POINT

Where are you emotionally here? What do you think of that person for not replying? If you're frustrated, is your frustration valid?

ⓘ ERROR WARNING

If you feel slighted, dismissed, or ignored, you're not alone. Most professionals interpret that behavior as inconsiderate or unprofessional. But All-Stars don't.

Why? Because All-Stars don't monitor their messages for reactions. They move on. They trust the other person may be busy, or thinking, or distracted—and they give them the benefit of the doubt.

Sometimes, the person really *is* gathering their thoughts. Sometimes they just forgot to send. Ever have anything stuck in "Drafts" in Outlook? You get it. Either way, assigning intent doesn't help. It hurts.

---

[18] Steven J. Stein and Howard E. Book, *The EQ Edge: Emotional Intelligence and Your Success* (Hoboken, NJ: Wiley, 2006), 34.

Reframing

This brings us to a crucial emotional skill: reframing.

In *The EQ Edge: Emotional Intelligence and Your Success*, Stein and Book use a method called ABCDE to help reframe your ability to "debate your initial emotions."[18] You can't stop your emotional reactions—but you *can* pause, question them, and test their accuracy.

PERFORMANCE POINT

When a strong emotion hits, do you pause and assess it—or take it at face value?

ⓘ ERROR WARNING

Professionals often place too much stock in their initial emotions. Recognizing this is the first step toward growth.

Top leaders frequently use the phrase "Don't make an emotional decision." What they mean is, "Don't act on the first feeling you feel."

That's what Stein and Book were getting at. All-stars operate from a place of emotional audit and control. That's not to say control won't include loud, passionate debate. Review the chapter on strategic communication where I describe my peer hotly contesting a position. Poor emotional expression would have been screaming derogatory names and remarks. And while he was loud and passionate, he was being honest with his emotions, yet not impulsive.

Emotional Intelligence Foot Fault

Need an example of poor emotional expression? Let me tell you a story that's not easy to revisit. It's one of the lowest points of my professional career.

I had become estranged from my direct boss. In hindsight, that was largely due to my failure to communicate professionally and strategically—refer back to the communication chapter where I discuss communicating with your superiors; I could have used that skill back then.

My distrust of my boss had escalated to the point where I was not submitting to his authority regarding various directions he'd given me, earning me a summons to a meeting with the company president—my boss's superior—with my boss also in the room with us.

I was fuming. A week earlier, my boss had met with me privately and said, "The president is upset with your performance." Quick aside, a leadership 101 piece of advice: Never use your superior's authority as a weapon to control direct reports. (We'll discuss that in my next book, *So You Wanna Be an All-Star Leader*.) Worse off, during that meeting a week prior, the president randomly called my boss's cell phone, who picked up, and they had an unrelated conversation, my boss never indicating to the president that he was meeting with me at the time. Then, from seemingly nowhere, while I was still standing right there, my boss asked the president, "So are you still upset with Jared?" I was nauseous and almost felt dirty that the president never knew I was standing there during the call.

Back to the president's office for my "intervention." The president actually seemed upbeat. Friendly even. We chatted casually. This confused me somewhat since I was told he was "mad" at me.

We generically discussed the importance of being a team and working together. But then he asked me, "Do you agree with where we want to go from here?"

It was clear they just wanted to move forward. Smooth things over.

But I couldn't hold it in.

PERFORMANCE POINT

What would you do? Nod and move on—or throw the emotional grenade?

ⓘ ERROR WARNING

Professionals often blindside their bosses with emotional outbursts. Others go to the opposite extreme and *never* speak up. Neither is All-Star behavior.

I didn't handle it well. I can't remember my exact words, but I delivered a passionate rant on trust and loyalty—and how they were a poor example of it, referencing what my boss had told me about the president's view of me and the "secret" phone call. The president, visibly surprised, asked, "Jared, are you saying you don't trust your boss?" Both he and my boss stared at me with anticipation.

Without hesitation, I responded, "That's exactly what I'm saying!"

H. A. Dorfman, a brilliant sports psychologist, wrote about managing emotions as a baseball pitcher: "Work out of your rational system, your brain—not your emotional system. You will dissolve reason by arousing passion."[19] My response in the President's office was devoid of all reason.

It can be argued that my behavior wouldn't even be considered professional. But if you're reading this thinking, *I'd never do that*, ask yourself these questions: Do you let your emotions simmer and fester? Do you hold grudges and say nothing?

Holding emotions in without expressing them may *look* more professional—but it's not All-Star behavior either. That's the recipe for passive-aggressiveness.

An All-Star should still act. Request a private one-on-one to address what you view as inappropriate behavior from your boss and communicate that it's hard to build trust that way—not detonate in a high-stakes meeting as I did. I at least owed my boss the opportunity for him to hear my complaint privately and to meet me where I was. I failed to do so. A moment that I replay many times over.

Conversations around emotional intelligence usually focus on *negative* emotions. But managing *positive* emotions matters just as much.

[19] H. A. Dorfman, *The Mental ABC's of Pitching: A Handbook for Performance Enhancement* (Diamond Communications, 2000), 93.

PERFORMANCE POINT

Do your colleagues or boss recognize your emotional highs and lows and adjust how they work with you based on those?

ⓘ ERROR WARNING

Many professionals are emotional roller coasters. If people know when to approach—or avoid—you based on your mood, you are *not* displaying All-Star control. Even if you're upbeat more often than not, you don't want to be someone who is known for their vacillating emotions.

As Dorfman reminds us, emotions alone—sometimes even positive ones—won't return effective performance. Take Stein and Book's strategy, and audit, if not debate within yourself, your emotional response to whatever is going on. That means when that person doesn't reply to your Teams message and you initially get frustrated with their disrespect, debate your initial belief and emotion and consider other non-offensive alternatives to their lack of reply. Determine what is most likely and valid. This will help you make sure your decisions going forward are well grounded. Invest some time to work through emotions if necessary, and you will not only be viewed as an All-Star who can manage tough scenarios; you will *feel* like an All-Star.

Emotions Self-Reflection

This self-evaluation is for *you*. If you want to share with a trusted peer or leader to build accountability toward your newly acquired skills, that is a bonus. At the very least, if you are choosing to make a run at being an All-Star, personal accountability can start here. Decide which number below applies most to you at this point and circle the number.

1. I don't try to read a room, and I believe my feelings are my truth and people are going to know exactly how I feel, or I rarely let people know where I am emotionally.
2. I'll be honest: I see where I could improve in this skill as I've never really monitored my or other people's emotions in the workplace.
3. The professional behaviors and "errors" in this chapter best describe how I approach this skill. I am generally aware of my emotions or others, but sometimes I either lose my cool or get passive-aggressive.
4. I relate more to the All-Star skills, behaviors, and actions with regard to handling emotions at work. I am both controlled and assertive. People know where I stand, yet I consider myself approachable even when working through challenges.
5. I've been doing these All-Star actions with my emotions for at least three to five years.

The Closer – Bullpen Bullets

- ★ **Pause and reframe:** The next time a strong emotion hits, stop, breathe, label the feeling, and ask yourself if the automatic interpretation is accurate before you act.
- ★ **Give the benefit of the doubt:** When a colleague doesn't respond or seems inconsiderate, assume competing priorities or context you don't have and follow up calmly rather than assigning intent.
- ★ **Audit your emotional highs and lows:** Regularly reflect on how your moods affect colleagues and adjust your responses to remain consistent, professional, and effective. Don't be the roller coaster.

9

PLANNING

This is the chapter most will skip.

In the movie *Deepwater Horizon*, Mark Wahlberg plays Jimmy Williams, who says, while attempting to stop his company from a risky decision, "I don't hope for the best. Hope ain't a tactic."[20]

Congratulations, you've at least read two sentences in what is likely the most passed-over chapter of this book.

Let's dig in here, and be real with one another: Few people really derive joy from planning. As you likely know, I'm a big fan of Patrick Lencioni—especially his recent work on what he calls Working Genius profiles.[21] I won't get into the weeds on geniuses, competencies, and frustrations, but planning is absolutely a tenacity-style task. It also takes invention and discernment.

---

[20] *Deepwater Horizon*, Matthew Michael Carnahan and Matthew Sand, directed by Peter Berg, featuring Mark Wahlberg (Summit Entertainment, 2016).

[21] Patrick Lencioni, *The 6 Types of Working Genius: A Better Way to Understand Your Gifts, Your Frustrations, and Your Team* (Matt Holt Books, 2022).

In Patrick Lencioni's model, at one point or another, you're likely frustrated with the process of planning. For people who are tenacious and need to finish things, planning never feels finished. For those who like to invent or create or ideate, planning is extremely administrative and tactical.

Now, there are a rare few—people I absolutely admire—who skipped every other chapter just to read about planning. I love having these types of friends and peers to work with.

All that said, planning is a skill and requires a method. And if you do it consistently, it's one more notch in your All-Star belt.

Planning Fail

To be honest, planning is a clunky skill for me. It doesn't come naturally, and I have to work at it. Since entering the corporate world in 2011, I've been able to hold my own on the planning side of things, but I have had my moments of dropping the ball. Not enough to ruin my credibility, but enough to remind me how important planning is for anyone aiming to be an All-Star in their organization.

One of these slipups happened shortly after I started my stint at the firm I'm currently with. I had been in the role for about four or five months, and I was working on a project with the head of marketing. We were walking into a report-back meeting with our CEO.

I normally follow a pretty standard planning routine before I deliver significant content in a meeting. But on this particular day, for whatever reason, I had stacked back-to-back meetings and was essentially walking into this report-back meeting with zero preparation or research. I remember the day before, I stared at my calendar and figured I'd spend the evening prepping. Either my schedule or fatigue got the best of me because I didn't do it—probably convincing myself I'd just wake up early and prep in the morning. I didn't.

PERFORMANCE POINT

What do you do in this scenario if you are the key presenter in a meeting? Fake it till you make it? That's a common cliché in the office.

ⓘ ERROR WARNING

Professionals will do their best regardless and likely do so in this scenario as well, planning or not. All-stars will consider their meeting attendees and respect their time if they missed the mark, then communicate their circumstances to the most senior person who will be attending the meeting to see if the group needs to adjust the agenda. The bigger the group, the more difficult it will be to adjust.

So there I was, minutes before the meeting started, realizing I'd done very little planning or research. I had no real way to show any progress on the project, and the whole time, I was wondering how I could avoid sounding like I was just repeating what I said at the previous report-back.

Bear in mind, I knew the questions my CEO was likely to ask. But I hadn't built in the time to research and plan for them. These weren't surprise questions; he hadn't handed me a list or anything, but as I researched the project, I could tell what the barriers and challenges were going to be. I also knew that with time, he would discern those and ask about them. My job was to have the answers and the solutions. That required planning.

So when the questions came, though none of them surprised me, I didn't have solid answers. I reached for every cliché:

- "That's a good point. Let me look into that and I'll circle back."
- "Yes, we thought of that. There's a few more things we need to look at, but I'll follow up."
- "I'll need to get back to you on that one. I've got a few questions emailed out that will help me answer it."

This is NOT an All-Star move. I sidestepped every question the CEO asked. Worst of all, the head of marketing sat there awkwardly, fully aware of what was happening—I could tell by her expression that she knew I was unprepared.

The unproductive meeting ended. Seconds after I got back to my office, my CEO walked into my office, shut the door, and said, "You weren't prepared for that meeting, were you?"

I replied honestly, "No, sir. I wasn't."

One of the best things about my CEO is how he delivers feedback—quickly, clearly, and in a Brené Brown "clear is kind" kind of way.

He said, "Days like these will happen. What you should've done was offer us the chance to reschedule—just be honest and tell us you didn't have time to prepare. Then we could have made a decision whether or not we should reschedule or work through some of the detail during the meeting."

What was brilliant about that feedback? He didn't even have to address the circumstances that created the lack of planning. Instead, he focused on the courtesy owed to others when your lack of planning affects them.

This moment—while not career ending—instilled in me the importance of intentional planning.

PERFORMANCE POINT

What is your typical process for planning for a meeting, whether you're presenting a good portion of the content or even if you're there to get an update?

ⓘ ERROR WARNING

Professionals fall short of being All-Stars when it comes to planning. Many rely on past knowledge or prepare only by reviewing the content they'll present. Others don't prepare at all if they're not speaking—confident in their ability to "wing it."

Let me offer you a tactic: For any meeting, even if you're not the presenter, review the agenda and scope. All-stars protect their time more than anything else. If a meeting isn't prepared or doesn't have a plan, you need to ask, *Should I even be in this meeting?*

Often, I'll ask, "Is this a meeting I need to attend?" Sometimes the response is, "You can come if you want. We're just introducing some items, and we can follow up with you." That's when I'll choose not to attend.

If you are responsible for the material, here's a practice I encourage: a 1:1 planning ratio. For every minute of presentation or meeting time, spend one minute preparing. That's after the slide deck (if used) and agenda are done. Use that time to rehearse, anticipate questions, and prepare for objections.

A skill I see lacking in professionals is the ability to answer predictable questions. They'll say, "How was I supposed to know they'd ask that?" But if you're qualified to present, you're qualified to anticipate. What are the challenges? What have others tried? What's gone wrong in the past? All of those are predictable, and you can research the answers.

All-stars ask peers, "What questions did you face when you did this?" They research. They prepare.

If you're reading this and thinking, *I've never planned like this before*, don't worry—you're not alone. Most haven't. But the All-Stars in your organization plan this way. And you can decide whether to join them in this skill.

In one of my keynote talks, I share executive feedback about my ability to handle the boardroom. One executive said I was never surprised by a question or topic. That's not because I'm a genius; I am far from it. But I am rarely surprised, because I anticipate; I prepare.

Ritz Readiness

There's a book I recommend: *Excellence Wins* by Horst Schulze.[22] It's underappreciated. Probably because Schulze's view on work is so others-focused that it clashes with today's "have it my way" culture.

[22] Horst Schulze, *Excellence Wins: A No-Nonsense Guide to Becoming the Best in a World of Compromise* (Zondervan, 2019), 121–27.

Schulze champions a service mentality. That might sound like it only benefits the Ritz-Carlton industry or top executives, but that's not his message. Excellence, as he describes it, is rooted in planning and preparation—knowing what's coming so you're not surprised. At The Ritz-Carlton, Schulze implemented brief, daily stand-up meetings at the start of each shift. During these meetings, leaders would focus on one of the company's 24 service standards. They would read one of the standards aloud, discuss its meaning, and invite employees to share a relevant story illustrating the standard in action. This practice ensured that every employee, regardless of their role, was aligned with the company's service philosophy and understood how to apply it in their daily work. With a preparation method such as keeping those standards top of mind, the likelihood of failure to execute a standard was lower when they encountered a situation relating to one of the standards.

In the office, nothing screams unprepared louder than tech issues. We all know software lags. PowerPoints freeze. HDMI cords go missing. But these problems usually stem from a lack of planning. People blame the tech when really they started prepping two minutes before the meeting was supposed to start.

All-stars don't have tech issues. Their slides are up. The sound is working. Why? Because they cleared their schedule thirty minutes early and did a full technology check. That's planning.

One of the best examples of the All-Star planning I teach is how to work a room at a networking event. The firm I'm with now is amazing at planning for happy hours.

Yes, happy hours.

Professionals think happy hours are for free cocktails. All-stars know better.

They get attendee lists. They target who they need to speak to—clients, prospects, executives. Our execs are so dialed in that we even space them out in the venue to maximize engagement. We run pre-meetings before the happy hour. And yes, consumption is controlled—All-Stars treat it like work, not play.

PERFORMANCE POINT

At your last happy hour, networking event, or conference, did you review the attendee list or try to find out who was attending? Did you know who you wanted to catch up with?

ⓘ ERROR WARNING

Most professionals know the location of the happy hour, maybe the host company's name. That's it. If that's you, no shame—you've earned your way there. But don't confuse that with being an All-Star happy hour attendee.

Lastly—and most importantly—plan for people. Whom will you be interacting with, and what have they been going through? I won't dive into the emotional side of this (refer instead to the previous chapter on emotions), but proper planning makes you better in moments you didn't expect.

Matthew Pollard, in his book *The Introvert's Guide to Networking* lays out a phenomenal blueprint for planning for networking events like happy hours.[23] As an extrovert, I read the book anyway because I felt like any tools I could add to my toolbox would give me even more of an edge.

I'd be remiss if I didn't give a shout-out to some of the People Operations team I'm proud to lead. They crush All-Star planning. One even told me they prep for meetings with me by asking each other, "What questions do you think Jared is going to ask?" That's All-Star level performance.

Each of them shows up prepared. Not to dump every detail but to ask for decisions, provide updates, or move things forward. They know how to be All-Star planners.

[23] Matthew Pollard, *The Introvert's Edge to Networking: Work the Room, Leverage Social Media, Develop Powerful Connections* (HarperCollins, 2024).

The CEO Moment

There was one single most impactful moment in my early corporate career. I can confidently say this exchange with my CEO changed my career trajectory. The CEO had barely been in the seat for a year. As a manager, I was still three levels away, so our interactions were always cordial but sparse. I wasn't in "the circle."

Let me set up the scenario. I knew my way around recruiting. Frankly, there isn't much difference between recruiting college baseball players and recruiting corporate professionals. It's about relationships, communication, and caring. I had confidence in my sourcing and recruiting skills. I knew the business development division had been trying for months to upgrade their executive personnel. With relationships I had already cultivated in the business, I believed I was far inside six degrees of separation of finding someone; I just needed the green light to go hunting for the talent. I solicited this to my superior in almost every department update in a diplomatic check-in on the situation, but he always seemed dismissive of these solicitations. "They have external recruiters [headhunters] and a different strategy," he told me, never indicating he would suggest my willingness to the CEO who was driving the initiative. And he never further indicated what the "different strategy" was. I knew I was a little buried in the organization due to the stagnant style of some of the leadership above me, so I get it if you feel like you're in muddy shoes. Just keep developing and making All-Star moves—they pay off!

PERFORMANCE POINT

Do you give up asking or creating opportunities to use your talents when you are told no?

ⓘ ERROR WARNING

This is an inflection point for *many* professionals. A point of change. Professionals who feel stuck below poor or passive leaders need to understand the ceiling could be just a plateau—the point at which they are about to launch if they continue to work at All-Star levels.

You may feel there is no way to blast off your career when all you want to do is hustle and perform and your leader tamps your drive. Or worse, you may not even notice that you are dying on the vine because you believe your leader is doing it the right way by being passive and not an All-Star themselves. I'm glad you picked up this book. All-stars believe they can create opportunity regardless of the direct superior's organizational position or their effectiveness, or lack thereof. You just need to do it ethically and aboveboard.

Back to the CEO story. Later in the fourth quarter, I was tasked by the chief human resources officer to create a raise assessment presentation for all the chief officers of the company that would enable the executive team to review raise recommendations for their employees. While many HR practitioners would see this as a mundane task, very common for my skill set, I saw it as a huge opportunity. This was the first deliverable of mine that would go in front of every chief officer; plus, this was an opportunity to approach the CEO about this specific project's objectives. Normally, going "above" two levels to get answers is a CLM (career-limiting move) if you are not careful. However, approaching the CEO to discuss a project was reasonable in this case because the CEO himself originally requested this data, so seeking his preference on how he wanted the data organized was a logical move.

PERFORMANCE POINT

Do you seek opportunities to touch base and converse with executives in your company?

ⓘ ERROR WARNING

Professionals have a tendency to believe the hierarchal structure of companies is fixed for *every* form of communication and decision. But that's not always the case. Instead, focus on building rapport with your executive officers; it doesn't matter how many levels they are away. This is leveraging the All-Star skills of planning and relationships as best as possible. Executives are human too. If you read this and you're saying, "Not any of my officers, Jared; you just got lucky," then you are very much the same as the other employees in the company who worked for the same CEO I did. If you hesitate to approach higher-ups because you are socially uncomfortable or because you are socially awkward and do not want to risk their perception of you, then find a close confidant who will be straight with you about where you may seem awkward, and then work on those skills. If you do this, then be proud of yourself for giving an All-Star effort.

Our CEO, Jimmy Staton, had his door open. "Jimmy *(he insisted anyone in the company address him by his first name),* do you have a minute to talk about the raise information for next week's raise meeting?" The door was open, and he is an "open door" guy. I take people like this at their word, that their door is truly open, but I still *planned* this exchange.

"Sure, Jared, what do you need?" he welcomed.

I sat across from him at his desk and got right to the point, respecting his time. "I was going to split the recommendations up by division so each officer could present, but I wanted to make sure I had the information in a format you preferred."

Barely half a second passed.

"Bell curve," Jimmy quickly replied. "Then the top and bottom ten percent of each division, but don't label them as top and bottom; just list the highest and lowest recommendations. I don't like putting labels like top and bottom on people." No wonder this guy is a massively successful leader.

I affirmed, "I understand, no problem, I can do it."

With the objective of the ad hoc meeting accomplished, I quickly pivoted. "So how are you doing?" I asked.

"Oh, just great, things are running well," he exclaimed.

PERFORMANCE POINT

Would you have left at this point? He answered my questions and exchanged a little small talk and said everything was great.

ⓘ ERROR WARNING

If you leave, you didn't *plan* well. Many professionals find themselves in these moments but haven't planned adequately to take advantage of opportunities to brand themselves. All-stars prepare for high-value moments and opportunities even when they don't know when they'll happen; that takes thinking and caring.

I knew beforehand exactly what I wanted to *ask* Jimmy if I ever got to sit with him for five minutes. I believed I could bring value; I just needed the chance to offer it.

So here it is, the moment that changed everything.

"So . . . how are you really doing?" This time I asked more intently, at least hinting at empathizing with the chaotic life of a CEO when they are still new to a company. I held my eye contact so he knew I was interested in his heart, not small talk.

Jimmy got vulnerable quick. "We need revenue, Jared. We're doing fine financially and we're healthy, but we can be so much better. The business development consultants that we're trying aren't working out." These consultants were contractors responsible for helping us bring new money to the company. He mentioned them like I knew what he was talking about; this was probably the "different strategy" I was previously dismissed with by my boss. Jimmy continued, "We need to bring in someone at the executive level, a vice president, to build the business. I'm thinking about turning the recruiting over to your team."

Let's pause right here. No, I had no idea we would get here in this moment. I may have dreamed this would happen, but I couldn't believe what I just heard. But I was prepared. Shocked, but prepared. All those prior solicitations to my superior were because I had planned for the opportunity.

Sidebar: Remember the connections I made at the late-night BBQ dinner at the customer meeting, which I mentioned in chapter 1 on presence?! Those relationships were made and built over four years at that point. Four!

So I offered quickly. "I've got a few people in that space I can call right away to see who may be interested in talking with us."

"Yeah," he said, "I think I'm going to have you do that."

Assertively but respectfully, I said, "Well, do you *think* ... or do you *know*? Because I'll get on the phone right away." Yes, I said that to a CEO; my heart was racing because I had just put a decision on his lap, and it was a little terrifying.

He stared at me for what seemed like ten seconds but was probably one. I figured he was thinking either I was a cocky punk or I had some guts and was connected in the industry.

Jimmy, just as confidently, said back to me, "I know. Let's do it."

You may be thinking, "I could never do or say that." You can; you just haven't prepared, planned, and practiced. Those were not "off the cuff" moments. Okay, maybe the "Do you think or do you know?" part was quick on my feet. But I wanted an answer; I desired action on where I knew I could bring value. Not another idea that "we'll think about" and let fade away. If you want to be an All-Star, someone different than most professionals, you have to think, prepare, and be assertive with the skills and talents God has given you.

The book of Nehemiah in the Bible tells the story of who I think is the greatest professional transformed into a high-ranking executive ever. It's part of what inspired me in that moment with Jimmy. In chapter 1, Nehemiah planned and prayed for three months, getting ready for an opportunity if the king he was serving would just give him a window.

Three months! When the king asked what was on Nehemiah's mind at the beginning of chapter 2, Nehemiah was ready and the story of his success follows (Nehemiah 1–2:9).

If you had any executive in the country read through the above anecdote with Jimmy and me and asked your executive, "Can we do that here?" I imagine they would quickly say, "I wish everyone did that here." Executives want planning and assertiveness. This country is starving for it, and it is getting less and less common.

Professionals do a great job at what they are asked to do, and they check with their boss anytime they have a question. You can always stop there and have a pretty good career. Pretty good. All-stars, on the other hand, think and plan for bigger moments.

Here's the truth: If you're not planning, you're hoping, and just so we are crystal clear, "Hope ain't a tactic."

Planning Self-Reflection

This self-evaluation is for *you*. If you want to share with a trusted peer or leader to build accountability toward your newly acquired skills, that is a bonus. At the very least, if you are choosing to make a run at being an All-Star, personal accountability can start here. Decide which number below applies most to you at this point and circle the number.

1. I've never recognized or valued planning in the workplace. I only plan personal things.
2. I'll be honest: I see where I could improve in this skill, and I don't normally do even what professionals do when it comes to planning.
3. The professional behaviors and "errors" best describe how I approach this skill. I could plan much better with more intention.
4. I relate more to the All-Star skills, behaviors, and actions with regard to planning at work.
5. I've been doing these All-Star actions with planning for three to five years.

The Closer – Bullpen Bullets

- ★ **Plan intentionally for every meeting:** Review agendas, anticipate questions, and, if necessary, rehearse answers to ensure you're fully prepared and can add value.
- ★ **Leverage networking opportunities strategically:** Check attendee lists, identify key people to connect with, and set goals for meaningful interactions before events.
- ★ **Seek high-value moments proactively:** Identify opportunities to engage executives or decision-makers, plan your approach, and act assertively to contribute solutions or insights.

10

FRIDAY FOCUS — Avoid TGIT Syndrome

No professional will ever admit this, but ironically, every executive knows it: Thursday is the new Friday. You can palpably feel a "Thank God it's Thursday" (TGIT) feel in most offices now. I still find it odd when someone tells me to "have a good weekend" as they leave the office on Thursday.

The only way I can make sure this chapter ages well is by acknowledging the fact that there's a potential that one day it'll be common for more businesses to be closed on Fridays than not. I think we're a few years—if not ten—away from something like that, but let's not act like it's not already being talked about.

If you're reading this and this has already happened, no need to keep reading this out-of-date chapter. Unfortunately, you missed your window to become a very noticeable All-Star in your organization for very little extra effort.

But if you do have a business that's still open on Friday, this very well may be the easiest way to be seen as an All-Star: Adopt a "Friday focus" while actually working the hours that a professional would. Due to the simplicity of this concept, this chapter is the shortest—also somewhat ironic.

I imagine a good percentage of people reading this chapter get to work from home on Fridays, which is fine. But I'm going to encourage you to consider not running as many midday errands or getting trapped watching reels or shorts during the open parts of your calendar. Everyone knows this happens. It's easy to do, especially because there's a good likelihood that many of your bosses have already started their weekend vacation. They're out of the office too. And frankly, there's just not a lot of oversight on work on Fridays. At the very least, and knowing what we learned from Hutson and Rodriguez in chapter 2 on personal appearance, wear real shoes instead of house slippers; your mind and body need to know when it's "time to work."

I'll tell you this—I get a lot of stuff done on Fridays, and I love it. I do take a little bit of a competitive edge toward my workday, but I'm proud of my work. So when I know peers and others around me are taking their foot off the gas on a Friday—because it's Friday—and they feel justified because they've worked hard Monday through Thursday and earned the right to ease up, I keep my gas pedal down like it's a Tuesday. All the way until the end of the day, when I'm actually *supposed* to take my foot off the gas.

To be completely humble and vulnerable, have I ever cruise-controlled on a Friday before? Of course I have. That's why, when the lackadaisical part of me begins to take over on a Friday, I'm reminded that, frankly, I'm not doing right by my organization if I don't finish the week strong.

I always find it interesting what real, hard deadlines do to the days of the week. They make the name of the day not matter. If there is an absolute must-have by Friday at the end of the day, then the deadline is the focus, regardless of the day of the week, because the day of the week is not what matters; the work does.

Overhaul

I had the privilege—if not the honor—of leading a team of natural gas compressor operators. Typically, once a year, these operators would have to do major preventive engine maintenance on our compressor engines. Just imagine the engine of your car being the size of a two-car garage, height and width—and that's what they had to do preventive maintenance on. The work included changing spark plugs, checking pistons, taking measurements—essentially opening up the engine, inspecting it, and closing it back up.

It sounds easy until you realize these engines normally have natural gas running through them at about the speed of sound, somewhere in the neighborhood of 1,200 to 1,800 pounds per square inch of pressure. This creates much more wear and tear. And the tools to do the work are just as big as the engine is to a normal-size engine.

Anytime this maintenance is done, the company has to bypass that engine and send the gas down a different pipeline so the engine can be safely opened. This puts a strain on the pipeline because you need these engines to hold pressure in order to push the gas down the pipelines to communities and businesses that need the natural gas. You can only do this type of maintenance for a certain amount of time before it creates problems upstream. These problems can result in engines upstream shutting down because the natural gas backs up, creating a domino effect.

The team I led had some of the busiest engines on the pipeline. Our company didn't like having those engines down very long because of how much pressure it put on the line. Our section of the pipeline—in natural gas terms—was known as a "major constriction point." In the grand scheme of things, what that means to the end user—the people who purchase the gas to heat their homes or generate electricity—is that when we shut one of those engines down, they no longer get the same amount of gas for a certain period of time. Which means we can't sell as much. And where my team's engines were located in the pipeline system, there wasn't another place to pull natural gas from to substitute for what was missing.

So the longer those engines were shut down, the less money the business made. And nobody likes to run a business like that.

Most teams would get two weeks to do these engine "overhauls," because in their areas of the pipeline, there were other gas sources to pull from. Our team? We were normally given five days. And when I say five days, I mean five days—because the customer fully expected to be getting their natural gas again by day 6, which was most often a Saturday.

Fast-forward to a Friday during an overhaul—around five p.m.—and the team was feeling great. We were on track to be home by dinner, with the maintenance wrapped up; that was a great feeling because the team typically worked long days to stay on track and make sure we were done by the end of the day on Friday.

One of the last things you do before closing out an overhaul is spray soapy water around the engine's cylinders and pistons to check for leaks while it's back up and running at full blast. In my time there, that always seemed like an exercise in futility—because by then, everything was sealed tight. But it was on the checklist.

Well, as you might guess, when one of the cylinders got hit with the soapy water, air bubbles started flowing like a bubble bath. We all looked around, trying to figure out who had jinxed us by talking about leaving on time.

Finding a leak at that point meant every Friday plan we had was gone. It was all hands on deck and me ordering pizza for the crew that night.

I won't go into all the technical detail and how we worked through the rest of that Friday, late into the evening, but I can assure you, that engine was running before midnight with no leaks.

PERFORMANCE POINT

Do you work all the way through Friday—or ease up halfway through if you have no external deadlines?

ⓘ ERROR WARNING

If you answered "halfway through," you're right alongside most professionals. With the majority of professionals still "working from home" on Fridays, the temptation to work on anything but actual work is immense. This is an error many professionals continue to make—and they miss opportunities to make All-Star moves in their organizations.

Build your own "pipeline overhaul deadlines" that drive the completion of tasks. If you have a light day, then find executives who are in the office on Fridays. Grab lunch or coffee with them. Learn about their goals, objectives, or ways you can innovate to help them.

Make no mistake: There *are* executives in the office on Fridays. You just have to seek them out. That's the focus you must have on Fridays if you want to join the All-Star ranks.

Jim Collins, in his timeless book *Good to Great*, references Level 5 Leaders—those who are fiercely determined.[24] Find one and watch how they work on Fridays. Don't assume they "started" working like that once they got the title. And let's be clear—this isn't a "work–life balance" issue. This is about finishing the work we're all paid to do. This is about working through Friday.

The Last Light

My first executive role was for a company in western Kentucky. On Fridays, I typically left the office around five thirty, give or take depending on my goals for the day. In western Kentucky, because it's so close to the Eastern time zone but still Central, it starts getting dark around four thirty. By five thirty, it's basically night.

I'd walk out of the office to my lonely Chrysler 300, which only an hour earlier was surrounded by neighboring cars. In a big, dimly lit lot, only the company cars were parked in the background and a couple more left from a few shift employees who worked twelve-hour days.

---

[24] Jim Collins, *Good to Great: Why Some Companies Make the Leap . . . And Others Don't* (Harper Business, 2011).

As I turned out of the property, I could see the front of the building. One obvious light was usually still on, illuminating the side of the building. I could make out the profile easily—our chief financial officer. Still sitting at her desk. Still being an All-Star. A Level 5 Leader. Fiercely determined. Working *through* the Friday.

This skill is not "for show." You should have your to-do list firmed up so you can work through the last day of the week and accomplish your goals for the day. You shouldn't ever find yourself at work with "no work."

PERFORMANCE POINT

As you read this, can you think of something you could accomplish in the next hour that would be considered work*? Something that would knock off a to-do or advance a project you're currently on?*

ⓘ ERROR WARNING

Many professionals don't necessarily know about—nor do they particularly have—a backlog or list of things they could do for their role right now. If you're in this situation, you either need to dig into your department and see what's available to work on or, dare I say, ask for additional responsibilities from your superior, because as it is, you don't have enough responsibilities to be an All-Star.

If you're short on to-dos, you need to build a backlog. Maybe something from another chapter in this book—something around innovation or relationships. And barring a deadline like our pipeline operators had, when you're done, you're done. But have a Friday focus and work through the day.

I had a great benefits analyst who would get to the end of a day and say, "I've reached the point of diminishing returns." This was the point at which he had worked so fiercely that his focus and efficiency wouldn't return what it could if he were fresh. Staying an extra fifteen minutes wouldn't deliver more than it was worth. But he always worked through the day—hard and dedicated—no matter the time of day or day of the week.

As I said at the beginning of this chapter, this is actually the one area of your work life where you can gain All-Star status and no additional effort beyond what you're already paid for is required. That's just the nature of the workforce in the current climate. Professionals get idle on Fridays. All-stars find another gear. This is the easiest opportunity to work an honest eight hours and be seen as far ahead of your peer group.

Friday Focus Self-Reflection

This self-evaluation is for *you*. If you want to share with a trusted peer or leader to build accountability toward your newly acquired skills, that is a bonus. At the very least, if you are choosing to make a run at being an All-Star, personal accountability can start here. Decide which number below applies most to you at this point and circle the number.

1. I'm not convinced working hard on a Friday will make a difference, and I like relaxing at home anytime I can work from home.
2. I'll be honest: I see where I could improve in this skill by working through Fridays instead of taking advantage of the lack of oversight. I often plan errands and work on personal things on Fridays.
3. The professional behaviors and "errors" regarding having a Friday focus best describe how I approach this skill. I work pretty hard until lunch and maybe an hour more, but I tend to coast on Fridays.
4. I relate more to the All-Star skills, behaviors, and actions as described in this chapter; I often work in the office or harder than most of my peers on Fridays.
5. I've been doing these All-Star actions with regard to having a Friday focus for three to five years.

The Closer – Bullpen Bullets

- ★ **Maintain full focus on Fridays:** Treat the day like any other workday, avoiding distractions, errands, or early wind-downs to complete meaningful tasks.
- ★ **Build and leverage a Friday backlog:** Identify tasks or projects that advance your work and tackle them proactively when your schedule feels light.
- ★ **Seek out executive interactions:** Use Fridays to personally connect with leaders, ask questions, and offer solutions, taking advantage of the lower-traffic opportunities in the office.

ACTION AND FINAL SELF-ASSESSMENT

There you have it. Ten skills you can focus effort on tomorrow if you desire to become an All-Star in your place of business.

You may decide that it's not quite the season or in your goal bucket to make the run for promotions, and that is okay. Companies and organizations are built on solid professionals.

I desire, though, that each of you who has read about the skills in this book realize that the decision makers in your companies are not looking to promote someone who does their job, comes in right at opening time, and starts packing up two minutes before closing time.

Executives are looking for the ones who always seem to be one step ahead of the pack, whatever the job, task, event, or unforeseen challenge. Executives are looking for All-Stars. Are you the next one they'll find?

On the next page, input the scores you gave yourself during each of the chapter self-reflections. Then add them together to get your overall total. A scoring guide follows for your overall score.

After assessing, it's now in your hands. I recommend taking two or three skills we focused on, and at a minimum employing a couple of the bullpen bullets at the end of the chapter into your behaviors and decisions. Then as those become more routine for you, grow in the other skills. However you decide to work these skills into your career journey, don't just wanna—go become an All-Star.

Self-Reflection Total:

1. PRESENCE ________
2. PERSONAL APPEARANCE ________
3. RESOLVE ________
4. RELATIONSHIPS ________
5. GRATITUDE ________
6. COMMUNICATION ________
7. INNOVATION ________
8. EMOTIONS ________
9. PLANNING ________
10. FRIDAY FOCUS – Avoid TGIT ________
11. **TOTAL** ________

Total Score Key

46–50 **Hall of Famer** – When All-Stars are All-Stars year after year, in sports or celebrity, they will end up in the Hall of Fame. These are the All-Stars of the All-Stars. If you have had all these skills mastered for three to five years, you are likely one of the executives of your company or one of the "high potential" employees who others assume will be in an executive office soon. Congratulations!

40–45 **All-Star** – Welcome and congrats; your organization very likely already views you as an All-Star and has "plans" for you. If you don't know this, you need to ask and find out what those plans are so you can lean into them in your future development. Hone in on the areas that were a 3, if any, and shore up your All-Star status.

35–39 **Solid Professional** – Great for the organization, valuable contributor. If you decide you want to level up and go for the All-Star ladder-climbing status, go for it! If you are good being a great professional, congrats and thank you for doing what you do!

30–34 **Professional** – Valuable contributor to the organization. Your executives likely don't expect you to fly off the page or they don't have you on the succession planning list, but your value is not in question. If you are desiring to grow, you should now know actionable steps you can take tomorrow.

25–29 **Developing** – You've got some action items to start getting into the professional status and a road map if you decide you want to be an All-Star. If you really want to make a run at it, determine what areas you desire feedback on and seek out that feedback from a superior who has these skills; they will appreciate you for it.

<25 **Deciding** – If you scored yourself honestly here, screenshot your chapter list and total score and email it to me at jared@hamiltonexecutivecoaching.com, and I will offer you a fifteen-minute free consult. Going to be direct, you need to make a decision if the place you are working is motivating you to be a professional, let alone an All-Star. You either have indifference or major blind spots. I am happy to discuss.

ACKNOWLEDGMENTS

I'm going to reference all the people who made this book possible by their first name, and last initial if there are multiple.

Steph, cousin and publisher, I still remember the day in your living room when you commented on one of my first corporate trips to headquarters, "They are going to fast-track you." You saw in me these skills, and this book, before I could ever think it possible.

Whitney, Jules, Jadei, Will, and Wes, the only way this was possible was you all being an All-Star family throughout this book journey, I needed your love and grace more than you know. You all are the absolute inspiration. I love you (and all our pets).

Mom and Dad, you've sat at the table for years and prayed together; you've seen challenges faced and so many prayers answered. Here's another. Thank you and I love you.

Heather and Jason, Operation CF, you are faith warriors and the big sister and brother who believed in me when few would.

Tom, Tanna, Sean, Jesse, and Heather (outlaw), there are very few "in-laws" who benefit from the kind of absolute unconditional love that you all consistently "show up" and bring. I know I am in rare company. I love you all.

Uncle Roy and Aunt Maryland, Rockdale is responsible for a good chunk of this book. It is a writer's paradise. You are some of the most generous people I know. I love you all.

Pastors Q, Steve, Brian, Jordan, John, and Bob; thank you for always discipling and praying for me. Thank you to all my small group prayer warriors and Ms. Katie proofing over vacay.

My career would never have been possible without my work teams at Moundridge USD, Buhler USD, Central Christian, Sterling, Havasu/ Haysville Heat (Rick/Chief), Southern Star, and Calvetti Ferguson. There are so many of you I still text here and there, I fear I would miss someone; I have a special place for all of you in my heart.

Special nod to Donald, Kelly S, Travis, Lance, and Kelly R for welcoming me on a cold fall day in Colby.

A shoutout to my HR teams that have made so much of this possible; Sharon, Michelle, Mary Beth, Angie, Zac, Jeff, Steph Q, Mandy, Eva, Hailey, Claire, Taylor, Sophie, and Nic. My leaders throughout the years; Jerry M, Jerry A, Dave F, Andy, Paul, Stacy and David F; I've learned so much from each of you. And Gary, the letter of recommendation in 2011 was a pivotal moment. Thank you.

Finally, the executives that have mentored and directly or indirectly helped shape this book for the next generation of All-Stars; Gayle, Commander Rob, Brett, Tami, Kevin, (Coach) Jim C, Lori, Cary, Nicolas, Glen, John B, Rob E, Tracey, and thank you for the 90 seconds Denis. Jimmy and Shawn, the hours you spent mentoring me, even after my move has inspired me more than you know.

Liz and Rod, I could write a page; but if I 'have' to be an HR nerd; you are two I'd need in my club.

Sarah, Shibu, and Jason D; thank you for spending some of your holiday reading and offering testimonial. You are All-Stars!

I can only ask for forgiveness if I missed someone; I will get you on the next book (wink emoji, Lu).

ABOUT THE AUTHOR

Jared Hamilton is a people-first leader, executive coach, and culture builder whose professional journey spans more than two decades across athletics, energy, and professional services.

Jared's path to executive leadership wasn't a straight line. His career began on the baseball field, where he served as head baseball coach and athletic director at Central Christian College of Kansas, then later also as head baseball coach at Sterling College of Kansas. Coaching young athletes taught him lessons that would anchor the rest of his professional life—discipline, teamwork, accountability, and the transformative power of belief. He learned early that talent alone doesn't make a player great; consistent effort, emotional control, and leadership do. Those lessons became the foundation of how he would later lead teams in business.

After years in collegiate athletics, Jared transitioned into the corporate world, joining Southern Star Central Gas Pipeline, a company with nearly six thousand miles of natural gas transmission infrastructure across the Midwest. Over nearly eight years there, he quickly rose through leadership roles—in field operations and human resources—overseeing complex people operations, leadership development programs, and large-scale organizational initiatives. He quickly became known for his ability to connect operational performance with human performance, bridging the gap between front-line realities and executive strategy.

In 2019, Jared joined Calvetti Ferguson, a leading accounting and advisory firm headquartered in Houston, Texas. Over the next several years, he helped shape and scale the firm's people operations strategy. As CPO, Jared designs initiatives that elevate leadership capability, fosters engagement, and drives accountability through culture.

Alongside his corporate work, Jared launched Hamilton Executive Coaching, where he partners with executives, emerging leaders, and professionals who aspire to grow beyond competence—to become unmistakable "All-Stars" in their organizations. As a board-certified coach (BCC), Jared brings together years of business leadership, coaching experience, and psychological insight to help clients unlock performance through clarity, mindset, and communication. His coaching philosophy emphasizes authenticity, emotional intelligence, and professional resolve—the ability to stay committed when circumstances get difficult.

What makes Jared's approach distinct is that he doesn't just teach leadership; he's lived it in diverse environments. From college athletics to pipeline operations to boardrooms, he has consistently led teams through change and growth. His credibility comes from experience, and his guidance comes from empathy. Colleagues describe him as a leader who develops leaders—someone who sees potential before others do and creates space for it to grow.

Outside his professional life, Jared is deeply committed to faith, family, and lifelong learning. He resides in Texas, where he continues to coach, write, and mentor emerging leaders. Whether he's helping an executive navigate a career transition or watching a young professional take their first leadership step, his mission remains the same—to help people perform at their highest level while staying grounded in who they are.

Jared and his wife, Whitney, live in Houston, Texas. They stay busy keeping up with their four kids, Weston, Will, Jadei, and Julianna, serving at Cy-Life church and looking for a few hours here and there to sit by the pool.

THE
ALL STAR
PLAYBOOK
Drawing Up Your Fast Track to Promotion
COMPANION
WORKBOOK
to "So You Wanna
Be An All Star"
JARED HAMILTON

HAMILTON
EXECUTIVE
COACHING

Services provided:

- Executive & Leadership Coaching
- Emotional Intelligence Assessment & Coaching
- Working Genius Assessment & Coaching
- Team Building

Find out more at **hamiltonexecutivecoaching.com**

Follow Jared on social media **@the.real.coachham**

Connect with Jared on LinkedIn **@jared-hamilton-bcc**

www.ingramcontent.com/pod-product-compliance
Lightning Source LLC
LaVergne TN
LVHW051058210926
848486LV00024B/418/J
* 9 7 9 8 9 9 3 2 4 5 9 0 4 *